BEHIND ENEMY LINES

UNDER FIRE IN THE MIDDLE EAST

BY BILL DOYLE

SCHOLASTIC INC.

NEW YORK   TORONTO   LONDON   AUCKLAND
SYDNEY   MEXICO CITY   NEW DELHI   HONG KONG

FOR ALL THOSE STRIVING FOR FREEDOM BEHIND ENEMY LINES
— B.D.

ISBN 978-0-545-33463-1

12 11 10 9 8 7 6 5 4 3   11 12 13 14 15 16/0

Printed in the U.S.A.   40
First printing, September 2011

CONTENTS

BRAVING THE NIGHT

One of the greatest challenges in writing this book wasn't finding brave men and women with amazing, action-packed stories of courage to share. You have only to look to the soldiers serving in our country's military to discover daily acts of heroism and selflessness. With such possibilities, the biggest difficulty was narrowing down the list.

Focusing on modern conflicts in the Middle East, Afghanistan, and Pakistan, the eight true stories of bravery and courage collected here include a young corporal rushing into a blazing fire to save a team member, a special ops soldier swimming through dark waters to defuse a bomb, and a flight medic risking his life to rescue an enemy fighter.

These incredible heroes are real. For security and storytelling purposes, scenes have been dramatized, some locations changed, and events shaped and combined. In nearly every chapter, the names of people — other than the main subjects — have been changed. While each of their thrilling experiences is extremely different from the next, two common threads tie this collection together.

First: War takes a toll, and in ways that are not always obvious. Many of the soldiers described in this book have continued to show courage off the battlefield by seeking help for both the physical and emotional impacts of war. Still, most of these heroes have no regrets. "Even after all of the suffering I went through," says the sergeant described in "Demon Platoon," "I would do it all again for the love I have for my country."

Second: War zones are always dangerous places, but when the sun goes down, they can be even more terrifying. Soldiers must rely on all of their senses to spot the enemy, avoid traps, and stay alive. At night, they're more vulnerable to threats that lurk in the darkness. But while others might have retreated or cowered in the shadows, these courageous individuals shone even more brightly.

In fact, all the heroes in this book had a chance to play it safe or give up trying to help others. But they didn't. Rising to the challenge, they prove to us that glory is not in the violence of war, but rather in the unfailing human spirit — the one that says, "I will not turn my back on freedom and my fellow man, not this night . . . not ever."

— BILL DOYLE

DEMON PLATOON

WHILE OTHERS RUN FROM EXPLOSIVES, ONE ARMY SERGEANT SEARCHES THEM OUT IN A TERRORIST-FILLED CITY IN IRAQ

"No, no, go away!" the old Iraqi man shouted as he slammed his front door in the face of Army Sergeant Tim Faust.

Out on the dark street, Tim stepped back and signaled his men to move on to the next house. He knew not to take the old man's response personally. After all, the terrorist group al-Qaeda had issued a warning to the forty thousand people of Hit: "If you help the Americans, we'll kill you and your family."

Years of conflict had taken their toll on the Iraqi city, tearing it apart. Piles of crumbling bricks and garbage covered the streets. Al-Qaeda terrorists had hidden hundreds of improvised explosive devices, or IEDs, in the debris or buried the bombs underground. Fear hung over the city like a thick fog.

But Tim was here to help change that.

For the past three months, he and his sixteen-member Demon Platoon had been hunting down and destroying the al-Qaeda IEDs — mines, artillery shells, and other explosives — along the main supply route through the city.

Snipers often shot at the Demon Platoon as they cleared the route used by U.S. military trucks and commanders. It was incredibly dangerous work, and Tim had already lived through explosions — he'd actually been blown up twice.

Tonight, just after ten P.M. on July 4, 2006, Tim and his gunner, Sergeant Greg Higgins, patrolled the shadowy streets, while the Demon Platoon cleared the route. The platoon was also tasked with knocking on doors to help recruit locals for the Iraqi police department. If Hit was going to be free of terrorists, the Iraqi people were going to have to take control of their own security.

The rest of Tim's platoon circled a two-block radius around them, ready to move in if any trouble arose.

So far, most of Hit's citizens, like the scared old man they'd just visited, had been too afraid to talk. Hoping for better luck at the next house, Tim led the way through an alley. His eyes scanned the trash and rocks on the ground.

"Great place to hide an IED if they really wanted to mess us up, huh, Tim?" Greg commented.

Tim nodded. "Keep sharp," he said. Then, in his head, he added a quick prayer: *Please don't let there be any IEDs here. And if there are, don't let anybody get hurt. And if anybody does get hurt, let it be me. And if it's me, don't let me get hurt so bad that I can't see my family.*

So far tonight, his prayer had been answered.

Then Tim's radio crackled with a call from his commander: "Demon Platoon, Eye-in-the-Sky has spotted two MAMs inserting possible IED in the ground at the intersection of Bronze and Cherry. Mission priority high."

Translation: The military's drone planes flying miles overhead spotted two "military-age males" burying explosives in the ground at a busy intersection near the market. Take care of it now.

Their recruiting efforts would have to wait. Tim relayed the information to the other members of his platoon. Within seconds, an armored Humvee zipped up next to Tim and Greg. Tim climbed into the passenger seat and Greg took his spot in the gunner's perch.

"Hey, Sarge, happy Fourth," said the driver, Specialist Paul Ferguson, with a grin.

"Independence Day," Tim said. "The perfect day to bring a little more freedom to this city. Let's just hope that there aren't any fireworks."

The Demon Platoon raced across Bronze Street and stopped just before it intersected with Cherry. The nearby shops were closed up tight and the streets were empty — except for two suspicious-looking men lurking on the sidewalk. Tim ordered two sergeants to detain them. Once they were secured in the back of a Humvee, Paul waved Tim over.

Pointing thirty feet past a beat-up storage shed, Paul said, "The Eye-in-the-Sky couldn't pinpoint the exact location of the IED. But I think I see it toward the other side of the intersection, and it looks like a big one."

To be safe, Tim ordered all of the vehicles to back up two hundred fifty feet. Then he turned to Paul. "Walk me a little closer and show me where you think the bomb is."

Slowly they made their way to the storage shed. A light dangled from the shed's roof, illuminating their every movement to whoever might be watching them. Tim smashed the lightbulb with the butt of his M-4 rifle.

"There's something strange about the garbage over there," Paul said.

Tim nodded. One reason Demon Platoon was so successful — they'd found 80 percent of the concealed bombs on their route — was because Tim had taught his men an important trick of the trade.

"Each time you go out, memorize everything you see on the street — trash, rocks, whatever," he'd told them. "That way, when you pass by again, you'll notice if anything has been moved. That's where the IEDs have been planted."

Now Paul directed Tim's eyes to a pile of garbage about thirty feet away, on the fringes of the intersection. Crumpled newspapers partially covered several crushed, white Styrofoam cups.

"I'd swear the cups there were on top of the paper when we came through last time," he said.

Tim focused his night vision binoculars. *There it is!* He saw part of a black bag with a small antenna poking out from it under the trash. It was an IED.

"Nice job, Paul," Tim said. "Head on back to the Humvees."

Paul nodded, knowing better than to argue. Someone had to get close enough to mark the IED's location. Tim would never ask one of his soldiers to do it. He kept the most dangerous jobs for himself.

After Paul left the area, Tim took a glow stick from the pouch on his belt. He snapped the stick so it lit up, and slowly moved closer to the IED. When he was fifteen feet away, he tossed the stick carefully. It landed inches from the bomb.

Now when the explosive ordinance detachment, or EOD, arrived, they could use the light to quickly spot and disarm the device.

Satisfied, Tim backed two steps away toward the Humvees. When his foot came down for the third step —

The IED exploded.

As always with an IED, Tim saw and felt the explosion before he heard it.

Out of the corner of his eye, he saw the ground rise like a volcano. Then he felt waves of heat wash over him. It was like standing in front of a thousand hair dryers blowing bits of shrapnel and debris into him. Finally, he heard the explosion.

BLAM!

By then Tim was flying through the air. The force of the blast sent him soaring twenty feet. He landed face-first on the hard road.

The protective gear he wore saved his life. Shrapnel dotted the back of his vest. Without it, that shrapnel would have torn through his chest. Other pieces cut through less fortified areas and ripped through his uniform into his legs.

Tim couldn't move his body or hear anything. Everything seemed to be in slow motion.

Tim saw his men taking cover and raising their weapons. The dirt around him exploded in a spray of gunfire as two enemy combatants shot at them from a nearby alley. The Demon Platoon quickly started firing back.

Up on the second floor of the building next to the alley, Tim spotted an open window. The triggerman who'd detonated the IED must have been standing up there. He had probably used a cell phone to send the signal that triggered the bomb.

After exchanging fire for thirty seconds, the men in the alley ran off, with Tim's soldiers in pursuit. Greg and a medic rushed over to Tim, pulling him toward the relative safety of the Humvees. Tim felt like his back had been hit with a sledgehammer. The sharp, instant pain told him that part of his lower back must be broken.

And the pain also snapped him out of his daze. As they carried him to the vehicles, Tim glanced at the crater left by the IED. It was big enough to swallow a Humvee, maybe two.

"How am I doing, Doc?" Tim asked the medic through gritted teeth.

But the medic wouldn't meet his eyes. The man's grim face said it all.

Hundreds of miles away, on a U.S. military base in Landstuhl, Germany, Tim Faust's wife, Laurie, was roused from a deep sleep by the ringing phone.

"Mrs. Faust, this is Captain Salmona," the army officer said. "I'm stationed here at the Landstuhl Regional Medical Center." He paused and then continued, "I'm sorry to inform you that your husband has been hit by an IED."

Laurie sat bolt upright in bed. "What?"

"The doctors in Hit don't expect him to live. He's being evacuated out of Iraq," the captain told her. "We'll take you and your kids to meet his plane so you can say your final good-byes when he arrives."

In shock, Laurie hung up, and then started calling family and friends to let them know the awful news.

Back at the U.S. base's aid station in Hit, the situation wasn't exactly as Laurie had been told. Tim had five herniated discs and three broken bones in his lower spine. But he was already up out of bed and moving around. He asked to use the satellite phone so he could check in with his wife.

"Oh, Tim, I'm so glad to hear your voice!" Laurie cried over the phone, nearly hysterical with happiness. "You're alive!"

Obviously, Captain Salmona had scared his wife for no reason. Angry, Tim went to find his doctor to chew him out for giving out false information about his condition.

"Son, I never sent any reports about you," the doctor said calmly. "That captain must have been repeating rumors. You can let him have it in person when you see him tomorrow. You're heading back to Germany."

Tim shook his head. "No, Doc. I can't go."

"What do you mean?" The doctor's eyebrows lifted. "You've been blown up three times since you've been here! It's time to take a break."

But Tim still refused. "I can't leave Hit. I've got to get back to work. The Demon Platoon needs me."

A year earlier, on his way to serve in Iraq, Tim had stopped in Germany to train a new platoon. He told the sergeant major at the German base, "I want to take over the worst platoon in the battalion."

"Why would you want that?" the sergeant major asked.

"Because then I can take them only one way," he answered. "And that's up."

The sergeant major obliged. He assigned Tim fifteen of the biggest renegades in the army. Some had minor criminal records.

"You're a pack of devils," Tim said when he first met them. "So I'm going to call you the Demon Platoon. I'll make you a deal: You do what I say, and we can keep each other alive when we get to Iraq."

Under Tim's guidance, the platoon blossomed in just six months. Their physical fitness test scores skyrocketed, and they began coming together as a unit.

By the time they got to Iraq, they were an organized, disciplined machine, ready to save lives by hunting down IEDs. And there were a lot of the explosives to find. The terrorists seemed to have an endless supply.

Yes, the Demon Platoon was working well together now — but they were still young and only halfway through their one-year deployment.

They still needed Tim, and that was why he wouldn't leave Iraq.

After the explosion, Tim's back was in excruciating pain. Still, the doctors had to argue to keep him in bed.

In the end, Tim only agreed to stay because a sandstorm also kept emergency aircraft grounded. Planes and choppers couldn't fly in the "red air."

"We wouldn't be able to evac you guys out in an emergency," a commander told Tim. "So you're all staying inside until the storm passes."

Tim knew al-Qaeda must be taking advantage of the red air. With the Demon Platoon stuck on the base, now was the perfect time for the terrorists to go out and plant IEDs.

When the red air finally cleared two days later, Tim and his platoon were itching to get back out on the streets and start clearing the route through the city.

"Is the EOD coming along?" Greg asked as they pulled out of the base in their Humvees.

"I requested that they follow behind us," Tim said. "It's going to be a busy day."

Tim took pride in never calling the EOD unless he really needed them. There was just one EOD team for the whole city, and he didn't want to waste their time. But he was sure they would find a lot of IEDs today.

With Tim's vehicle leading the way, they slowly inched along the beginning of the supply route. They knew the area from before the sandstorm and scanned the road for anything that wasn't there previously: disrupted dirt, new wiring, anything that seemed out of place.

"There!" Greg said, pointing at a small mound of household garbage. Paul rolled the Humvee to a stop nearby. Tim looked through binoculars to confirm what Greg had seen.

"Yep," he said. "There's an IED in there. Nice work, Greg."

Paul and the rest of the Demon Platoon backed up the vehicles to a safe distance. Tim marked the IED with a glow stick. Then he walked over and climbed into the rear of the waiting EOD truck.

"You can deploy the robot," he told Sergeant Nathan Vincent, one member of the four-person EOD team. The other three men lowered the robot to the ground. The machine resembled a mini-tank, with cameras and a long, multijointed arm sticking out of the front. As it motored away from the truck, the robot unspooled copper wire behind it.

Tim and Nathan gathered in front of a monitor that showed what the robot was seeing. As Nathan worked the remote control, they guided the robot toward the glow stick. The robot poked around the trash.

"There's the shell of the IED," Tim said, tapping the screen.

Nathan pressed a button, and the robot dropped a C-4 charge next to the IED. This charge was attached to the copper wire, and it would detonate the IED once they were out of range.

Nathan guided the robot back to the truck, while Tim scanned the area. Once Tim was sure that all the soldiers were safely behind their vehicles, he shouted, "Fire in the hole!"

Nathan pressed another button to detonate the C-4 charge and destroy the IED. A thirty-foot wall of fire shot into the air, and terrible thunder rolled down the street.

"That, my friends," Nathan said, "is what we call an IED."

The crew laughed. And then they began looking for the next one. It was going to be a long day.

A few IEDs were easy to spot. But many took serious scrutiny to find. To be safe, Tim carefully investigated each hunch, and about 90 percent of the time, he found an IED.

Every roadside bomb was different. Some could be triggered by cell phones or garage door openers. Other bombs had pressure-plate triggers — if anyone stepped on them or drove a vehicle over them, they would explode.

As the men worked, enemy gunfire often rang out from the rooftops. Tim's men would fire back until the terrorists ran off or were detained.

But even with the small, frequent attacks, the Demon Platoon and the EOD hit their groove. They'd find an IED, mark it with a glow stick, use the robot to drop the C-4, back the robot off, blow it, and continue along the route.

So far that day, the Demon Platoon had found twenty-one IEDs. A new record.

"There's number twenty-two," Paul said. He lifted a hand from the wheel of the patrol's Humvee and pointed toward the side of the road. A burlap sack covered two acetylene tanks strapped together with a round of rifle ammunition.

The IED was pretty obvious — at least to Tim and the Demon Platoon.

But clearly not to the soldiers in the three army Humvees cruising down the road toward them.

Tim snatched up his Humvee's radio. "Stop!" he shouted at the driver of the lead vehicle. "You've got an IED right in front of you!"

The driver's tired-sounding voice came back over the headset. "We've driven past that spot three times already today. It's nothing. We're —"

"I'm telling you it's an IED," Tim interrupted. "Stop your vehicles! Now!"

When the approaching platoon came to a stop, Tim got out to investigate. Sure enough, he found an IED. The EOD deployed the robot and they blew it up with the C-4.

As the explosion rumbled and echoed off the buildings, the driver of the other platoon turned to Tim. He looked a little sick.

"Thanks for stopping us," he said to Tim.

"No problem," Tim said. "It's what we do."

That day, Tim and his platoon were lucky. No one got hurt. Unfortunately, their luck ran out a month later.

It was midnight and Tim sat up in the gunner's turret of an M1 Abrams tank. Greg was down in the driver's hole. They were heading to one of Hit's busiest — and most dangerous — traffic circles. Terrorists attacked the circle constantly, but the platoon planned to keep the peace.

As they approached the traffic circle, Tim spotted something.

"There's a concrete barrier up ahead," he said to Greg over the headset. "Go around it, okay?"

"I see it, Sarge," Greg responded. He turned the tank —

And ran over two land mines stacked on top of each other.

The explosion blew the right track off the tank and the gun off its mount. It threw the sixty-eight-ton tank nearly sideways into the air. Tim was tossed to the turret floor, catching shrapnel in his left leg and striking his head.

The tank came back down and rolled forward. It crashed into the clock tower that stood in the middle of the traffic circle, and stopped moving.

For ten long minutes, Tim was trapped at the bottom of the tank's turret. His radio was out — he had no communication with Greg or the base.

Tim thought, *This time, I'm dead meat.*

If a terrorist climbed up the tank and popped a grenade down the turret, Tim would have no way of stopping him. He was stuck.

Finally, the authorities at the base realized what had happened and sent a quick-response team to pull them out of the wreckage. Greg was shaken up, but unhurt. Tim was taken straight to the aid station, where doctors examined him.

Just as he was climbing off the examining table, several members of the Demon Platoon rushed into the room. They looked worried about their leader.

"What'd the doctors say?" Paul asked.

Tim grimaced as he got to his feet. "If I get hit one more time, I'm going to have to get evaluated. That means leaving Iraq. And that's something I'm not ready to do."

"If . . ." Paul repeated with a small chuckle.

Tim nodded grimly. The Demon Platoon knew it wasn't a question of *if* he'd get hit, but *when*. It was simply part of hunting for IEDs. At some point, he would get blown up again.

Tim just didn't think it would happen so soon.

Three weeks later, the Demon Platoon was escorting the battalion commander's vehicle back to Hit after a visit with a local sheikh.

On the road ahead, Tim spotted a few potholes and guessed there would probably be an IED in at least one of them.

He grabbed the radio and called the battalion commander. "Sir, we're going to pull in front of your vehicle in case there are any problems up ahead."

Paul drove around the commander's vehicle to take the lead position. He swerved slightly to go around the first pothole, but didn't quite clear it.

The right front wheel rolled over a pressure plate that triggered an IED.

Tim felt the explosion that lifted the Humvee into the air, and then the world went dark.

When he opened his eyes, he was inside the base's aid station. The battalion commander stood next to his bed.

"Paul . . . ?" Tim asked. He was groggy; his head ached and his ears were ringing. "My men . . . ?"

Please let them be safe, he thought.

"They're fine, Sergeant," the commander said. "The Humvee, of course, is destroyed. That IED was meant for me. I want to thank you for taking the lead and saving my life."

The commander shook Tim's hand, and continued, "Now for the bad news. The doctor says you have the worst spine injury he's seen in his career, and he's recommended that you never see combat again."

Tim felt like he'd been punched in the stomach. What about the Demon Platoon? "Sir," he said, "I've got to stay here and —"

The commander held up a hand to stop him. "I'll make a deal with you. You go to Germany, and if the doctors there clear you, you can come right back."

Tim knew that probably would not happen. Once he was in Germany, they wouldn't let him return to Iraq.

The commander noticed the new look of pain on Tim's face. "Sergeant, you've been blown up five times in six months. You've had five concussions and your back is severely injured. Is this something you enjoy?"

Tim knew the commander was trying to joke with him and lighten the mood. But Tim answered seriously.

"A lot of people ask me why I'd volunteer for these missions," he said. "It has nothing to do with the adrenaline rush or the policies of politicians. It's all about the men on the left and the right of me . . . and bringing them home alive."

The commander nodded, clearly impressed by Tim's words. "Well, now it's your turn," he said. "You're going home, Sergeant."

In 2006, the army awarded Tim Faust the Bronze Star, four Purple Hearts, the Army Commendation Medal with valor, and the Combat Action Badge for heroism, meritorious service, and extraordinary achievement. He was promoted to master sergeant. In 2007, Tim and his family returned to the United States. Tim had four back surgeries and was diagnosed with traumatic brain injury. He fought to stay in the army, but in 2009, he was medically retired. While it was hard leaving behind a twenty-year career, Tim fills his time writing and working with troubled teens who have been expelled from high school. He helps them pass their GEDs and get their lives back on track.

ESCAPE FROM IRAQ

IN A DESPERATE BID FOR FREEDOM, FIVE MEN HELD CAPTIVE IN IRAQ STEAL
AWAY ON A SMALL LIFE RAFT, INTO THE DANGERS OF THE PERSIAN GULF

"Hurry up!" Jean-Claude Departe whispered. "The soldiers will
be here any second!"

"I'm doing my best!" Mike Teesdale spun the old-fashioned ham
radio's dials and threw its switches. But it wouldn't power on, and
they were running out of time.

"Let me have a try," said Preston Watt, the third man crowded
inside the small radio room.

Nearly blind, Preston's eyes swam behind the thick lenses of his
glasses. He ran his hands over the radio parts and secured a loose
clip on the battery.

"There, that should do it," Preston said with a quick nod.

Mike tried the power again. This time the radio lit up and the
gauges danced. He clapped Preston on the back, and then turned to
Jean-Claude. "You're on."

Jean-Claude sat in front of the radio and put on the headset. He
toggled the switch to transmit, and said in French, "This is S6A-BAT
calling TV3-JKS."

If the Iraqi military were monitoring the airwaves, they'd hear the call sign of a ham radio user in Singapore. Of course, the call sign was a fake, meant to throw the military off track. The three men in the radio room — along with two other colleagues — were trapped in the port city of Basra in Iraq.

They had come from Great Britain and France to work for a marine loading company in Basra for ten weeks.

But a month ago, in August of 1990, Iraq had invaded its neighbor Kuwait. Tensions between Iraq and surrounding nations, as well as Western nations, rose. And although official war with the coalition of the United Nations had not yet been declared, the Iraqi government had restricted the movement of many foreigners in the country. Mike and his coworkers had become prisoners. They were confined to the company compound, and the Iraqi military had locked them out of the radio room.

That morning, desperate to contact the outside world, the men had hatched a plan. Two of them would distract the soldiers by pretending to be sick, while the other three picked the lock on the radio room and called their company headquarters in Paris for help.

And that was just what Jean-Claude was doing on the radio now. Mike could speak a little French and got the gist of Jean-Claude's transmission. The company said it would find a way to send money to the men. They could use it to bribe their way out of the compound and, hopefully, out of the country.

"Merci." Jean-Claude signed off and got to his feet. "Let's go."

"Wait a second," Mike said. He took Jean-Claude's place in front of the radio.

"No!" The Frenchman pulled on Mike's arm. "We have to go. If the Iraqis catch you, they'll make all of us pay."

Preston stepped between them. "Come on, Jean-Claude," he said. "Mike will be right behind us."

Once Preston and Jean-Claude were gone, Mike used the false Singapore ID again. He called the ham radio in the basement of his house, a world away in Kent, Great Britain.

Mike's fourteen-year-old son answered on the other end. "Go ahead, Singapore."

At the sound of his son's voice, Mike's heart leapt. He hadn't spoken to his wife or two children in a month. "Son, it's your pop."

"Dad? Is that really you?" his son cried. "Where are you? We've been worried sick."

"I'm okay." Mike didn't dare say more in case the Iraqis were listening. "Are you — ?"

Mike heard a door down the hallway squeak open, and the sounds of soldiers' voices headed toward the radio room.

"I'll get Mum," his son said over the radio. "She's out in the garden — Mum!"

The soldiers' voices in the hallway grew louder.

"There's no time, son," Mike said softly. "I love you. Tell your mother and sister I love them."

"What, Dad?" his son asked. "I can't hear you!"

"I hope to see you soon," Mike whispered even more softly, not sure if his son could make out his words. He clicked off the radio and removed the headset.

But before Mike could leave, footsteps pounded down the hall outside the door. Mike had waited too long. The soldiers were here! And there was no way out.

But maybe there was a way . . . up.

✳

An instant later, the big, bald Iraqi soldier Mike had nicknamed Bull and a second, skinnier security guard burst into the radio room. They looked around, behind the door and under the desk.

They found no one, and spoke to each other in hushed, urgent tones. Bull pointed to the lock on the door, clearly blaming the other soldier for not locking it.

Unseen for now, Mike lay on top of a filing cabinet. He'd squeezed himself between the cabinet and the suspended tiles of the ceiling. He'd jammed a box against his stomach for camouflage.

As the men continued to speak, Mike felt the box shift with each breath he took. The rise and fall of his chest was pushing the box. It was going to tumble to the ground — and he would be caught!

He risked a quick breath, and felt the cardboard box slide an inch closer to the edge of the cabinet. One more breath and the box would fall. Mike froze.

Bull said something to the other guard, and together they both headed for the door.

Wait. Wait, Mike told himself. *Don't breathe. Not yet.*

Just as the skinnier guard was leaving, static from his walkie-talkie filled the office. He stopped in the doorway, fished the radio out of his pocket, and barked a greeting. From the way his tone suddenly changed, it was obvious he was talking to a commanding officer.

Mike's eyes filled with bright stars and his lungs burned. He had to breathe! Finally the guard shoved the walkie-talkie in his pocket and left the office.

Mike let out the breath he was holding, grabbing the box just as it was about to tumble to the floor. He climbed down from the filing cabinet and poked his head out the door. The hallway was empty.

He snuck outside to the bright daylight.

"The Iraqis must know about the radio transmissions, Mike," Karl Morton groaned the next morning. Karl was one of the other workers from Great Britain.

Standing in the doorway of their barracks, he pointed to the small building that housed the radio room. It sat three hundred yards away, by a shallow river that flowed out to the Persian Gulf. The radio room had been sealed again, this time with three locks. And security had been stepped up. An Iraqi soldier now patrolled the area constantly.

"You did such a good job faking a stomachache to distract them, they don't suspect a thing," Mike assured him. "Besides, if the Iraqis knew we'd called the company, they'd have punished us by now."

But Karl wasn't convinced and groaned again.

Of the five men, Mike and Karl were the closest friends — and Mike could see that Karl was starting to go a bit stir-crazy.

When they had been free, Karl had been the confident captain of the supply ship that brought the compound's food and water. But after the Iraqis invaded Kuwait, they had confiscated Karl's ship, forcing him to live in the barracks.

Those first days had been rough on Karl. He missed his ship and the freedom it represented. Plus, the bombs exploding in nearby

Kuwait were taking a toll on all of the men. Their boss had called and told them to remain at work. Everything would be sorted out. In the meantime, they should keep doing their jobs until they were told differently.

So they waited. And waited. But soon Mike realized they had waited too long. The phones were cut off. Armed Iraqi soldiers built bunkers around the compound and fenced it in on three sides. The river on the fourth side led to the Persian Gulf and to nearby Saudi Arabia — but those rough waters were patrolled by the Iraqi navy. Besides, they didn't have a ship.

Their workplace had become a prison camp.

"The world's forgotten about us," Karl said, bringing Mike out of his thoughts.

Before he could say something soothing, a hand tapped him on the shoulder. Mike turned to find Alain Benoit, the second Frenchman in the camp.

"Chow time," Alain announced. He had taken up the cooking duties. But he was running out of food to prepare. They were down to a bowl of rice each per day — that and whatever Alain could scrounge up to throw in with the rice.

"What are we having today?" Mike asked him, his stomach growling.

"Ah." Alain tried to smile. "Rice mixed with a very, very light seasoning. It's called *air.*"

Twelve days later, the money from the company's headquarters arrived. Over two thousand dollars stuffed in a diplomatic pouch had traveled hundreds of miles from Paris through Baghdad along the back roads of Iraq — and finally to the prison camp.

Mike couldn't believe it. "Why would the Iraqis deliver a bag full of money?" he wondered out loud. "Why not just keep it?"

"The French embassy is still on decent terms with Baghdad," Jean-Claude answered. "The money came in a French diplomatic pouch. The Iraqis didn't want to risk upsetting the French by opening it. They already have enough on their plate."

In the end, though, all their efforts were for nothing. The money didn't make a difference. While they didn't dare try to bribe Bull, they did give the cash to the other guards. But these guards never followed through on promises to help.

Violence in the area grew. The men could hear explosions from car bombs — and gunfire from skirmishes between Kuwaitis and Iraqis — coming from the nearby highway. And the men's food supply was basically down to nothing. They each had a couple of spoonfuls of rice now at meals. That was it.

"Okay, buying our way out didn't work," Mike said to the men. "We need to find a different way."

The prisoners began meeting daily to discuss how to escape. The roads were no good. They were too dangerous with too many Iraqis patrolling the area. They considered swimming down the shallow river to Iran or Kuwait. But even if they didn't drown, the men weren't sure how they would be treated when they got there. They could be captured and held under even worse conditions.

No one could come up with a plan.

Then one morning Mike and Preston were walking to the Iraqi kitchen to ask for extra food. Bull and two guards sat in plastic chairs outside the kitchen door, eating platefuls of steaming beans and rice. As Mike and Preston approached with their stomachs growling, Bull ignored them and kept talking. The other guards nodded at everything he said as if terrified of him.

Bull rambled on in Arabic for a few minutes. Impatient, Preston cleared his throat to get their attention, but Mike was just listening. He knew a little Arabic and picked up the words:

Americans . . . Navy . . . growing . . . Persian Gulf.

Bull noticed Mike staring. The guard snarled something, which included what they all knew was a curse word, and waved a fist at Mike.

Mike took a step back. But Preston held his ground.

"I don't know exactly what you're saying," Preston said to Bull. "But I don't like it."

The two other guards' jaws dropped, and Bull slowly got to his feet.

Holding up one hand and pulling Preston with the other, Mike said, "No, it's okay. We're leaving."

"He can't talk to people like that, Mike," Preston protested as they headed back to their rooms.

"I'm glad he's talking like that," Mike whispered. "Let's get Karl and the Frenchmen. Bull might have just given us a way out of here."

"You want to take a tiny lifeboat forty miles down the river to the Persian Gulf?" Karl asked in shock. "And hope that we get picked up by the U.S. Navy?"

When Mike nodded, Karl threw up his hands. "Why don't we just jump on a pogo stick and hop our way there? It'd make as much sense!"

The five men sat in Mike's room, and Karl's voice was loud in the small space.

"We've been prisoners for almost eight weeks," Mike said quietly. "I think it's our only chance to get home."

"Ha!" Karl said. He pointed out the window toward the river where a bright yellow and orange life raft was strapped to the back of the crane's platform. An Iraqi guard leaned against the railing nearby.

"See those neon colors on the raft? The ones that scream, 'We're escaping! We're escaping!'" Karl said. "And what about the raft's deafening motor? It will make it impossible to sneak away from here and past the Iraqi naval base down the river!"

"I actually think the idea could work," Preston said as he rubbed his thick glasses on his shirt and put them back on. "Of course, we'll need to stockpile enough fuel for the trip and find a way to quiet the engine."

"One thing is for sure," Mike said. "We'll starve if we stay here." He looked down at his body. He'd dropped from 186 pounds to a shocking 130 pounds. His six-foot frame was all bones. "Soon we'll be too weak to escape."

This hit home with everyone . . . even Karl. He took a breath and said, "All right, let's do it."

Bull and the other soldiers always focused their attention on the road, never thinking the prisoners would be foolish enough to try a water escape. They left a single soldier to guard the crane platform on the water. And, each day after lunch, that soldier ducked out of sight to take an hour-long nap.

For five days, as the guard slept, Alain removed his sneakers and crept onto the platform to siphon fuel from the crane's engine. He handed the plastic gallon containers he filled to Preston and Jean-Claude. They tucked the fuel onto the life raft, hiding it under the seats.

Meanwhile, Mike and Karl hatched a plan to make the life raft's engine quieter. Just after lunch every day, they scavenged the material they needed from the crane. On the sixth day, their luck ran out.

Mike and Karl were just stepping off the crane platform with their stolen loot, when —

"You!" the sleepy-sounding guard called, sitting up in his spot in the shade. "What are you doing?"

Karl froze. Mike turned, but kept his hands hidden behind him. "Nothing," he stammered.

"What are you carrying?" The guard rubbed his eyes, slowly waking up.

Mike brought his hands around. They were filled with wads of pink, flameproof insulation he'd stolen off a gas pipe.

The guard's eyebrows shot up. "Why do you have that?"

"I'm cold," Mike lied, thinking fast. "I'm going to plug up the cracks in my room. Very drafty. *Brrr.*"

Cold in this heat? The Iraqi guard looked at him like he was nuts, and let them go.

The next day, they wrapped the insulation around the life raft's engine to muffle the sound as best they could.

They were ready. The seventh night after hatching their escape plan, Mike told the others, "We leave tomorrow at noon."

None of the prisoners was able to sleep that night. In the morning, Mike found Karl hunched over the toilet. He was sick as a dog.

"What's wrong with Karl?" Jean-Claude asked Mike. "Flu?"

"No, just nerves," Mike said.

Jean-Claude nodded, looking a little green himself. The thought of getting on that small boat and pushing out to the Persian Gulf was terrifying.

Karl emerged from the bathroom and guessed they had been talking about him. "All's well," he said. "There's nothing in this stomach to throw up anyway!"

This made them all chuckle. Together they finished packing up their few belongings and went over the plan a final time. A little before noon, Preston said, "I'll meet you at the raft in a few minutes. I have to run one last errand."

When the guard disappeared for his after-lunch nap, the other four men carried fishing rods out to the life raft. If any of the guards stopped them now, they would claim they were going fishing. But without bait or hooks, their story wouldn't hold up for long.

First they had to lower the life raft down to the water. Mike flinched as each tug caused the ropes to let out a loud squeak. When the raft was bobbing in the water, they climbed aboard. The life raft would be crowded, but at least it had a small roof on one side that could protect them from the sun.

The men looked up at the crane platform, waiting for Preston. They heard footsteps approaching and tensed. Was it the guard? A face peeked over the side.

"Preston!" Mike hissed. "You gave us a fright!"

"I thought we could use these to guide us," Preston whispered as he handed over some nautical charts. "I stole them from the storage shed."

He descended the platform's ladder and joined them on board the raft. They pushed away from the platform, and their journey toward freedom began.

The men waited until they had drifted about a hundred feet before trying to turn on the engine.

"Here goes nothing," Mike said, putting his hand on the starter cord.

Karl cringed as if he expected to hear a siren alerting all the Iraqis in the area to their escape. But as the engine whirred to life, it made only a low rumble. The insulation was doing its job.

They motored along for four miles. All was quiet. Then they came around a sharp bend and found themselves face-to-face with the gray hull of an Iraqi navy ship. It was anchored a hundred feet away, along with several other navy ships. Onshore, Iraqi sailors bustled about, loading and unloading cargo.

Mike realized the navy could easily sink them with one shot. Or, at the very least, he and the others could be detained and locked up in a real prison.

Karl's face looked pale. "We should have waited for nightfall. What do we do?"

Mike shrugged. There was nothing to do. They had to keep going. Everyone huddled under the raft's small roof, hiding from the shadows of the towering military ships that stretched out toward them.

"Did you know Sinbad the Sailor launched many of his sea voyages from Basra?" Preston said, trying to distract Karl.

No one said a word. They were too focused on the Iraqi ships' cannons. Mike waited to be spotted. But the navy either didn't notice them or assumed they were local fishermen. In either case, no one from the Iraqi ships made a move toward them.

When they were finally past the ships, Karl leaned over the back of the raft and threw up.

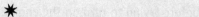

In the early evening, the shallow river opened up into the vast waters of the Persian Gulf. Iran sat on one side of them, Kuwait on the other, with Iraq at their backs, and endless dark waves in front of them. Which direction should they head?

Then Jean-Claude spotted the shapes of a few boats out on the horizon. Mike raised the binoculars he'd taken from the camp. "I can't tell what kinds of ships those are," he said.

"Better just to avoid them," Alain said. "Until we know for sure. That way —"

"There's no food in here," Karl interrupted. He was poking around the containers of fuel under the seats.

Mike had been waiting for this moment. He knew Karl would be upset when he made this discovery — there was no food on board because there hadn't been any left in the camp to pack. "Actually, there's a bottle of water in there," Mike said.

"There isn't any food? We'll starve!" Karl glared at Preston. "And don't start telling me about Sinbad again. Even he had to eat!"

By the time land disappeared behind them, their prayers for darkness had been answered. And then some. Only a sliver of the moon and a handful of stars managed to poke through the patchy clouds that hung overhead.

Without a flashlight, it was too dark to read their nautical charts. And without a compass, they quickly lost their sense of direction. As the sea grew rougher, wave after wave pummeled the raft, spinning it like a cork. They would fall into a swell, then rise up, only to find they were facing a different way.

The men looked to Karl to point them in the right direction. After all, he had been a ship's captain. But Mike could see Karl was too frightened to think straight. He sat stock-still with a dazed expression. His hands latched on to the side of the raft in a death grip as the boat bobbed up and down and the seawater sprayed them.

"It's okay!" Alain shouted above the wind, taking his turn steering. "I was in the French foreign legion. They taught us navigation skills. We'll keep the moon to the left and that bunch of stars just to the right, and then we'll be going south!"

For the next hour, they managed to move in a relatively straight line through the endless waves. Then, something slid past the side of the boat. In the dark, Mike thought it looked like a small oil slick. Then another one drifted by, and this time Mike recognized what it was. His stomach sank.

"We're floating in a minefield!" he said, as they passed another underwater mine just a few feet away.

Panic struck the men. Just one small bump against a mine and the raft could trigger an explosion that would kill them all.

"Stop!" Karl cried. The shock of the situation had yanked him out of his stupor.

"Not an option," Mike said. "If we turn off the engine, the swells could still knock us right into a mine. We have to keep motoring ahead. It's our only choice."

Karl clutched his stomach like he might be sick again.

"No!" Jean-Claude shouted. "Don't lean over the side — you might hit a mine!"

Fortunately, there was nothing for Karl to heave up. He just sat bolt upright, and moaned as the tiny boat pushed blindly through the minefield.

Preston tried to lighten the mood. "Want me to steer?" he asked, pointing at his thick glasses. No one laughed. They were too scared. Every second might be their last.

Just a short time ago, the men had prayed for darkness. Now they prayed for light.

Eight hours after they emerged from the minefield, Karl suddenly sat straight up. "If we're going south, that means we're heading to Kuwait."

Mike and the others realized he was right. If they arrived in Kuwait, the Iraqis could easily recapture them.

"We can't go back the way we came," Preston said. "That will carry us back into the minefield, and it's still dark out."

So Alain turned the boat left.

"Where are we going now?" Karl asked anxiously.

Alain's confidence as a navigator was blown. He just shrugged. "I'm sorry. I have no idea."

When the sun began to rise, the men were able to figure out that they were heading west. But there was no land in sight. They bobbed in the water for what felt like an eternity.

Ten hours later, their luck began to change. "There!" Jean-Claude said. "I see a boat!"

Mike waited for the life raft to rise to the top of a swell. Then he gazed through the binoculars. He spotted the ship. "There's no flag. Could be a military craft."

"What country's military?" Preston asked.

Mike didn't know the answer to that. But the pounding afternoon sun had driven the temperature sky-high. They had nothing to eat or drink. Mike didn't think he could bear another night on the sea.

"Enough is enough," Preston said, as if reading Mike's thoughts. "We've been out here for twenty-five hours. It's time for this to end."

Without any more discussion, Mike took the rudder and steered the life raft toward the distant ship. As they approached, Preston asked, "Well, what is it? Friend or foe?"

"I don't know," Mike said. "There aren't any flags."

But someone on the one-hundred-fifty-foot ship must have spotted them. Its engines stopped and ropes were tossed over the side. Mike steered the raft as best he could along the ship's hull, which rose like a towering gray wall.

"Grab the ropes!" Mike shouted.

But the tired, hungry men on the raft were almost too weak to hold on. As if the waves knew this was their last chance, they yanked the raft back and forth even more violently. One moment the raft was slammed into the side of the ship, and the next it was almost dragged away.

Finally, after nearly being tossed into the sea, the five men were all pulled aboard.

On deck, the ship's captain glared at them for a few seconds. When he finally opened his mouth, he turned to one of his sailors and rattled off a command in Arabic. "Call the navy. Have them send a boat."

Mike's heart skipped. He was sure they would be turned over to the Iraqi navy and taken prisoner again. They'd gone through this ordeal for nothing!

But the ship that cut through the waves toward them thirty minutes later didn't belong to Iraq.

"It's a Saudi boat!" Jean-Claude shouted happily. Saudi Arabia was a member of the coalition. The men quietly celebrated their luck. In a short time, they would be free!

The Saudis launched a dinghy with six soldiers aboard. They didn't know whether Mike and his friends were setting some kind of Iraqi trap, so the soldiers had their guns drawn when they boarded the ship. But the escapees must have looked pitiful in their wet shorts and T-shirts. They were all skin and bones — with nothing but their passports in their back pockets.

The lead soldier ordered the guns lowered and spoke to the men in English. "Not to worry," he said kindly. "You're a mile inside of Saudi waters. This boat that picked you up is one of ours." He turned his attention to their life raft. "What were you doing in the middle of the sea on such a small craft? Weren't you terrified?"

Sharing a look with the others, Mike said, "The minefield we went through was fairly frightening."

The Saudi chuckled. "You do realize that the path you chose took you through *two* minefields, don't you?"

Mike gasped. Somewhere in the night they must have traveled through the second one without even knowing it!

"We'll get in touch with the British and French embassies," the Saudi soldier told them, "and then get you home. But first, what would you like to eat?"

Next to him, Karl's stomach growled, and Mike's face broke into a grin. "Anything but rice!"

The Saudi soldiers allowed Mike to call home and tell his family he was safe. By that time, the press had found out about the prisoners' escape and there was a worldwide rush of attention. The British government debriefed Mike and his friends, hoping they might be helpful in describing Iraqi military positions. They were able to tell all they knew about the naval base and location of Iraqi ships, but Mike is unsure if action was ever taken based on that information. On January 16, 1991, three months after Mike Teesdale's escape, the United States launched Operation Desert Storm with an aerial attack on Iraq. Once Iraqi forces were driven out of Kuwait, the United States declared a cease-fire on February 28, 1991.

DIVING INTO FIRE

WHEN HER CONVOY IS ATTACKED IN IRAQ, AN ARMY CORPORAL CRAWLS INTO AN INFERNO TO SAVE A TRAPPED PASSENGER

"Ladies and gentlemen!" the announcer boomed. "Please welcome true American heroes to the 2008 Army All-American Bowl!"

Television cameras swooped around the stadium as the crowd of thirty-six thousand roared. They had come to San Antonio's Alamodome to cheer on the country's best high school football players. And, of course, to honor ninety soldiers who had served in Iraq or Afghanistan during a special halftime ceremony.

Sergeant Crystal Kepler was one of those soldiers. Right now, the petite twenty-four-year-old stood on the sidelines, waiting her turn to head out to the fifty-yard line to say a few words to the crowd. Even after all she had been through, speaking in front of people and sharing her story still made her nervous.

Crystal's mom was waiting with her and noticed. "Are you okay?" her mom asked, and squeezed her daughter's hand.

"I'm fine, Mom," Crystal said, touching the scars of burns on her neck. "I'm just thinking about how I got here."

Four years earlier, Crystal had been a typical twenty-year-old living in Glendale, California. After she graduated high school, she'd attended community college for a short time and tried living with friends. But Crystal missed her family too much, so she moved in with her oldest brother, Andrew, who helped her figure out what her next step should be.

"What do you want to do with your life?" Andrew asked her one night at dinner.

Crystal thought about it. "I'd like to help people. Maybe in the military. If you were me, would you join the air force or the army?"

"The army," Andrew said with a laugh because the answer seemed so obvious to him. After all, he'd served in the National Guard.

He wasn't laughing when Crystal came home the next day.

"I joined the army," she announced. "I stopped at a military recruitment office and signed up for four years as a health care specialist."

"A health care specialist?" Andrew's eyes went wide. "That's another way of saying combat medic! I didn't know you were that serious about the military. I would've stopped you!"

Crystal patted him on the shoulder. "I want to do this," she insisted. "It's my chance to help people who put their lives on the line for our country."

But Andrew wasn't convinced that Crystal had made a good decision.

What have I done? he kept asking himself over the next three weeks. The question was still on his mind as he drove Crystal to the airport to catch her flight to basic training.

"Don't go, little sister," he said and hugged her tight.

"You worry too much," she assured him, heading into the terminal. "It will be fine!"

But an hour later, Crystal wasn't so sure.

She looked out the airplane window, high over the clouds, and clutched her armrest. Crystal had never been on a plane or anywhere far away from her family. And now she was flying from Los Angeles to basic training in Fort Leonard Wood, Missouri. She was scared and already homesick.

When they landed for a quick stopover in Dallas, Crystal rushed into the airport terminal to call home. Her mom picked up the phone, and Crystal burst into tears.

"Just come back to Glendale," her mom told her. "Forget it and just come back."

Hearing her mom's voice helped Crystal pull herself together. "No," she said, feeling a little better. "I agreed to do this, and I can see it through."

Crystal got back on the plane and flew off to basic training.

She'd known training would be hard, but she hadn't anticipated just how hard. From day one, the drill sergeants strictly enforced a long list of rules that governed each waking moment, including every detail about the soldiers' appearance. All the women would have to wear the same clothes and hairstyles. The sergeants went through their bags and tossed out anything that might be a distraction. There was even a rule banning nail polish and hair products. Crystal knew she shouldn't long for such indulgences. But in her civilian life, they'd always helped her feel confident and ready to face the day. Going without them was tough.

"I can't believe I signed up for this!" another cadet said as they walked into the barracks together. "We can't have candy? Not even flavored cough drops?" She stuck out her hand with a smile. "Hey, I'm Janet."

Crystal shook her hand and the two became instant friends. Both women were a little over five feet tall, the smallest cadets in their training class. During the long road marches, Crystal felt that their legs had to work overtime to keep up with everyone else's.

But soon Crystal found her attitude changing. She felt relieved that she didn't have to dress to impress people. Without all of the exterior stuff to worry about, she started seeing people for who they really were. And, although the drill sergeants pushed them hard, Crystal and the other cadets were rewarded for being strong and for having heart.

By the end of the eight weeks, Crystal knew she had made the right choice. "This is the place for me," Crystal told Janet as they waited in line to receive envelopes with information about their first posting. It would tell them where they would be sent for the next four or five years.

"I loved basic training," Crystal added as they moved up in line. "I'm almost sorry it's over."

"So you want to do it again?" Janet asked, a playful gleam in her eyes.

"Okay, maybe *love* is a strong word." Crystal laughed. "Where do you think we'll be stationed?"

When Crystal signed up with the recruiter, she knew there was a chance she'd be sent to the Middle East. But many people kept their fingers crossed that they'd be sent to work somewhere safer — in a hospital at a base in the United States or Germany.

Janet ripped open her envelope. "I hit the jackpot," she said with a grin. "I'm going to Germany. What about you, Crystal? Where are you going?"

Crystal hesitated for a moment. Then she opened the envelope.

A year later, Crystal contemplated the dark two-lane highway that stretched out in front of her.

It was just after ten P.M. and she was driving the lead Humvee of an eleven-vehicle convoy. They were returning to Forward Operating Base Kalsu, or FOB Kalsu, an hour south of Baghdad, Iraq. The big trucks behind Crystal were loaded down with gravel and concrete blocks — materials they were moving to FOB Kalsu from FOB Duke, a base about sixty miles to the south.

After basic training, Crystal had gone to combat medic school. Since arriving in Iraq, however, she'd taken on many different kinds of duties. She was a soldier first and would do whatever the army asked. Her dedication and hard work had earned her a promotion to corporal.

Crystal missed Janet, but had made new friends in her unit. One of her pals, David Howard, sat behind the fifty-caliber gun mounted to the top of the Humvee. They were joined by Barbara Hanson, the lieutenant in charge of the convoy. She sat in the front passenger seat, and their Iraqi interpreter, Mustafa Ahmad, sat in the back.

Crystal had already made this trip six times. By direct route, it took two hours to get from FOB Duke back to FOB Kalsu. But the convoy would often travel up to ten hours out of its way to return to home base. The detours threw off enemies like al-Qaeda, who might be planning to attack the convoy. The convoy had taken this particular detour for the past three nights, and, in the back of her mind, Crystal wondered if they were making a tactical mistake.

Are we being too predictable? Are we an easy target?

Before she could mention her doubts to the lieutenant, she spotted the lights of an Iraqi checkpoint at the bottom of a hill up ahead. Tension in the vehicle went up a notch.

"Let's stay focused, people," Barbara said.

Run by the Iraqi police, the checkpoints were meant to make the highway more secure. But they could often be the most dangerous parts of the trip. If a corrupt police officer sold information to al-Qaeda terrorists, the enemy would know when a U.S. convoy was in the area and could prepare to attack.

With the cones and barriers restricting the flow of traffic, Crystal was forced to slow down. The Iraqi officer at the checkpoint saw them coming and waved them through.

Everyone in the Humvee relaxed a little as the convoy rumbled past the checkpoint and continued along the dark highway. Other than their headlights, the only illumination came from a few apartment buildings that dotted the sides of the road.

"Knock knock," David prompted over their headsets. Now that they were over a mile beyond the checkpoint, Crystal knew he was trying to break some of the tension with a joke.

"Who's there?" asked Barbara.

"Tank."

"Tank who?" asked Mustafa, the interpreter.

Before David could answer, Crystal spotted the lights of another convoy from their unit coming toward them. She flashed her Humvee's lights to let them know they were friendly.

"You're welcome," David said, delivering the punch line.

"I get it," Mustafa said drily.

"Then why aren't you laughing?" David asked in mock horror.

"Because it's not funny," Mustafa answered. Now Crystal and the lieutenant started laughing. And then —

Ka-BLAM!

The passenger window exploded in a burst of orange light.

Something rocketed toward them from the side of the road. Crystal knew it must be an explosively formed projectile, or EFP. The powerful bomb burst, slamming into the Humvee on the passenger side and instantly killing the lieutenant.

The vehicle's windows cracked, but battle adhesive kept them from shattering.

The blast blew the fifty-caliber gun off the top of the Humvee. The gun shot through the air and landed a hundred feet away. Fire and smoke poured from the right half of the vehicle. The attacker had loaded the EFP with coins, and now pieces of copper burned through Crystal's shirt into her skin.

Stunned, Crystal thought, *A truck from the convoy on the other side of the road hit us.*

Yet she knew that didn't make sense.

We have to get out of here!

She slammed her foot on the gas pedal, but the Humvee wouldn't budge.

David crawled out of the gunner's hatch, jumped off the roof, and landed on the road. Shrapnel wounds covered his legs, but he was lucky to be alive.

"Crystal, open your door!" he yelled.

Crystal's senses were scrambled. David was ten feet away, but she felt like he was just inches from the window. Everything around her moved in slow motion.

"Get out of the vehicle!" David shouted.

Still in a fog, Crystal opened the door. As she climbed out, her helmet fell to the dusty road.

I'm not going to put my helmet back on my head — it's too uncomfortable.

That thought snapped Crystal out of her daze. She wasn't thinking straight. *Not wear my helmet? That's crazy!* She grabbed it and shoved it back on her head.

"Are you okay?" David asked her. He led her away from the Humvee, while all the time his eyes danced along the windows of a nearby apartment building. "We have to move!"

Unlike an improvised explosive device, or IED, that detonated wherever it was placed, an EFP could be aimed. Someone had probably used a cell phone to trigger the bomb, waiting until the convoy was close and then dialing a certain number to set off the explosive.

The attackers could be up in one of the apartments along the road right now, watching them. Or they could be even closer, sneaking through the darkness toward the Humvee.

Ping! Ping!

The ammunition inside the burning Humvee was exploding, while still more shots rained down on them from one of the surrounding buildings.

"We need to take cover," Crystal said.

But when Crystal started moving, she didn't run away from the Humvee . . . instead she ran toward it.

Just a few seconds ago, the world had moved in slow motion. Now it was moving too fast.

Crystal reached the Humvee and leaned through the door she'd left open. The heat from the flames inside singed her skin and the smoke choked her. She could see that the lieutenant was dead.

Barbara, I'm sorry.

A hand reached from the backseat and grabbed her arm.

It was Mustafa! The explosion had pinned the interpreter's legs behind the front passenger seat. He was trapped. She couldn't pull him out through the front and the door closest to him was too mangled by the explosion to open.

"Don't leave me here, please!" he begged.

Crystal called up every ounce of strength she had. During her army medical training, her brain and body had been pushed to the limit. Her drill sergeants had taught her the skills she'd need to tend to the wounded at a breakneck pace. They had woken her up at three A.M. to go for five-mile runs in the dark to train her body to perform under duress. She had thrived on the challenges.

But this wasn't training. It was a real-life combat situation.

"I won't leave you," Crystal told Mustafa. She leaned back out of the Humvee, turned to David, and pointed to the back door on the driver's side. "We have to get Mustafa out through here!"

With David right behind her, she opened the door. She leaned back into the vehicle, and reached around the small ladder that led up to the gunner's hatch to get to Mustafa. He moved a few inches toward her — but that was all he could manage. His legs were still trapped behind the front seat. She pulled at his bulletproof vest, but couldn't move him any closer.

Through the smoke she could see his seat belt wasn't on. So what was holding him in place? His vest! The straps were hooked on a step on the gunner's ladder.

"Please hurry!" Mustafa shouted. The fire had spread. As the heat in the vehicle intensified, more of the Humvee's ammunition stores exploded and popped around them.

Mustafa's legs were burning. Without hesitating, Crystal crawled inside the Humvee to get a better grip on Mustafa's vest. She pulled as hard as she could, trying to free it from the step of the ladder.

Come on! Come on!

She didn't notice as flames licked and then burned the left side of her neck. All of her attention was focused on getting Mustafa out of the fire. She desperately yanked on the vest one last time.

Gotcha!

His vest — and then his legs — came free. Crystal pulled Mustafa over to the open door. David grabbed on to him, too, and together they dragged Mustafa out of the Humvee. With the enemy surrounding them, where could they hide?

Crystal scanned the area, and realized they had only one option. Quickly, they carried Mustafa fifteen feet to the side of the road where a ravine separated the lanes of the highway.

Kneeling down next to him, they threw dirt on Mustafa's legs to put out the flames. Crystal turned his body so Mustafa sloped head-first down the ravine's slight incline. Gravity would keep the blood flowing into his vital organs.

By now the Humvee was engulfed in flames. Mustafa would have died in the inferno. They couldn't go back in for the lieutenant's body. Not now. They would have to wait until help arrived. But when would that be?

Crystal looked up and down the dark road. She couldn't see a single vehicle from either convoy.

They were alone.

Of course, Crystal knew the two convoys were just following standard procedure. When one vehicle in a convoy was attacked, the rest of the vehicles had to get at least three hundred yards away to avoid the same fate.

Crystal put tourniquets on both of Mustafa's crushed and burned legs. It was clear that both limbs would have to be amputated from the knees down. But she needed to stop the bleeding.

"After that explosion, everyone must think we're dead," David said, crouching next to Crystal as she worked. "And we can't tell them anything different. Our only radio was in the Humvee."

"One of us has to go back to the checkpoint for help," Crystal said. "Mustafa needs to get to a hospital."

They decided Crystal should stay and keep treating Mustafa. David would follow the deep ravine that ran along the road back to their convoy.

"Do you want to take my gun?" Crystal asked. Since she always kept her gun slung around her when she drove, it had been with her when she got out of the Humvee. It was the only gun they had.

"No, you keep it," he said. "You might need it if any unfriendlies show up."

David crawled to the bottom of the ravine. "I'll be back as soon as I can!" he called up to her. "Stay tough."

And then he was gone.

"He's not coming back!" Mustafa said. "No one is coming to save us!"

"Shhh," Crystal soothed. "It's going to be okay."

Crystal knew Mustafa to be a good-hearted, college-educated man. But pain and fear had taken over.

Grabbing Crystal's arm, he cried, "We're going to die here!" As his hand squeezed, Crystal felt a jolt of excruciating pain.

Crystal looked down to find that she'd been hit. Adrenaline had masked the pain up until now, but a chunk of flesh was missing from her forearm. It had swelled up so quickly that she thought the bone might be broken.

Meanwhile, rounds of ammunition were still exploding in the burning Humvee, and gunfire pinged off the road around them. Someone was shooting at them from one of the nearby buildings. She knew — or at least wanted to believe — that the angle of the incline protected them from gunfire. But what if the attackers grew tired of just shooting at them, and came after them on foot? Mustafa and Crystal could be taken prisoner, or worse.

Crystal checked on Mustafa's tourniquets, and then lay down next to him. It would take David at least twenty minutes to walk back and get help. And with so many bullets flying around them, she wanted to stay as close to the ground as possible.

Now they would wait.

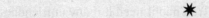

Twenty-five minutes passed. Still no sign of David.

Crystal kept assuring Mustafa that help would come. Inside, she battled her own growing fear. Her Humvee had been attacked, her lieutenant had died, Mustafa would surely lose his legs, and they lay stranded amid enemy fire.

Yet somehow, Crystal shrugged off her fear, and continued doing everything she could to make Mustafa comfortable.

Five more long minutes passed. Then ten —

"Crystal!"

It was the sweetest sound she'd ever heard. David was back! And he'd brought eight infantrymen with him.

"We're coming in," David called out. "Don't shoot."

Their shadows emerged from the darkness, and when Crystal saw them, she leapt to her feet. She couldn't wait for them to secure the area. Every second counted if they were going to save Mustafa's life.

"A helicopter is on its way for Mustafa," David said.

She gave him a quick nod of thanks, but there wasn't time to talk. They carefully lifted Mustafa onto a litter and rushed him back to the convoy.

When they arrived, Crystal ran to a vehicle toward the rear of the convoy, grabbed an IV bag from another medic, and sprinted back to Mustafa. As she hooked the IV up to the wounded man, a helicopter swooped overhead and landed on the road in front of them.

Crystal helped the chopper's medics get Mustafa on board. Then she insisted that David climb onto the chopper next to him. The shrapnel in his legs needed to be removed and his wounds treated.

"What about you?" David yelled into her ear over the sounds of the whirling blades. The chopper couldn't safely carry more than two patients at a time.

"I'll go with the quick-response team in a Humvee!" she shouted back. "They'll get me back to the base pronto." She patted David's shoulder. "I'll talk to you soon!"

She stepped back and watched the helicopter take off before heading to the trauma center.

"You okay to travel?" one of the members of the quick-response team asked her. The road ahead might be bumpy, and he looked concerned about the gash in her arm. But Crystal couldn't let herself think too much about it. She simply nodded and climbed into the team's Humvee. They rushed her to the nearest forward operating base, where she was greeted by an army major.

"I'm sorry about Lieutenant Hanson," the major said. "I know she was a friend of yours. And I know she would have been proud of what you did tonight."

Crystal nodded. "Thank you, sir." She would have to cope with these swirling feelings later.

"I was just about to call your mother to let her know about your injuries," the major said.

"Can I call her myself, Major?" Crystal asked.

He hesitated. This was not the way the army normally did things. Recently wounded soldiers weren't always emotionally ready to talk to loved ones. After a moment, though, the major smiled and nodded. He led her to his office. He pointed to a phone and left her alone. Crystal dialed the familiar number. She waited as the line rang and rang.

Then, a world away in California, her mom picked up the phone. . . .

"I'm okay," Crystal said as she squeezed her mother's hand. Her thoughts returned to the present. Two years later, she was back in the States, standing on the sidelines of the Army All-American Bowl. She had scars on her neck and arm that reminded her of the night she'd almost died.

"I'm so proud of you," her mom said.

Crystal gave her a quick hug as the announcer called her name. "Please welcome Sergeant Crystal Kepler!"

The people in the stands jumped to their feet as an American hero walked to the fifty-yard line. Crystal was ready to tell her story.

The day after the attack, a mechanic in the battalion asked Crystal if she wanted to see her burned-out vehicle, which had been brought back to the base. The only thing that remained of the Humvee was her seat. But some good came out of the wreckage. The mechanic was Landis Kepler, the man she'd eventually marry. Crystal Kepler received a Purple Heart and two Army Commendation Medals for her service in Iraq. The attack on her Humvee only reinforced Crystal's desire to help people. A month later, she reenlisted, adding two more years to her contract to work in the high stress of the emergency department. She is no longer in the service, but thinks of her "brothers and sisters" from her unit in Iraq often.

DUKE'S DOGS

THREE STRAY MUTTS LEAP INTO ACTION WHEN A BOMBER THREATENS AN ARMY SERGEANT AND FIFTY OTHER SOLDIERS

Just after nine o'clock on the night of February 11, 2010, a man slipped through the security gates of the U.S. army base in Dand Patan, Afghanistan. Dressed as a local to blend in with the traffic flowing in and out of the base, the man walked closely behind a supply truck. Too closely. When the truck jerked to the side, the man jumped away and his heavy backpack scraped against the gate's stone wall.

"You!" a voice shouted in English. The man froze. Had he been discovered already?

He turned to find an Afghan guard. *Of course*, the man thought. While this was an American base, about one hundred fifty Afghans lived on the compound. As part of a U.S. training program, this young soldier had been assigned guard duty. Luckily, the guard was still inexperienced and unsure of himself. He gave the intruder a long look.

"Be more careful," the guard finally said in Dari, the local language. Then he turned to inspect an approaching jeep.

"Good advice," the man replied. He did need to be more careful — or he could accidentally set off the twenty-five pounds of explosive C-4 in his backpack. He quickly scanned the compound, searching for his target. *There!* He crept toward the barracks that housed the fifty U.S. soldiers who lived on the base.

As he approached, the bomber could see through the window of the barracks door. Five soldiers sat in the main hallway, working on computers or talking on the phone — one of them reached down to pick up a pen he'd dropped on the floor.

That soldier has no idea that these are the last seconds of his life.

Once inside, the bomber would trigger his explosives. Setting them off within the barracks would cause the most damage.

The bomber placed one hand on the detonator under his shirt, and reached for the handle of the door with the other.

That was when he heard the dogs growling.

Inside the barracks, twenty-seven-year-old Army Sergeant Chris Duke picked up the pen he'd dropped on the floor of the hallway and turned his attention back to the computer screen in front of him. After a long day of teaching the Afghan border police about weapons and tactical planning to help fight terrorists, Chris was surfing the Web and checking his e-mail. Three of his fellow Georgia National Guardsmen tapped away on the computers next to him and another was on the phone.

The long, six-foot-wide hallway ran the length of the barracks. With doors to bedrooms, bathrooms, and offices opening on either side, the hallway housed computer stations and telephones for the soldiers to use, and they often congregated there.

"Hey!" A voice called from the front door and made Chris jump. But it was only one of his roommates, Staff Sergeant Ryan Edmunds.

"Let's go, Chris!" Ryan called. "Movie time!"

The room Chris shared with three other soldiers was down the hall, the one right next to the entrance to the barracks. Ryan and another of Chris's roommates, Staff Sergeant Scott Mulvoy, had been hanging out and playing *Call of Duty.* Video games had never really been Chris's thing. So nearly every night, Chris would wait for his buddies to finish playing, and then they'd all watch a DVD together or hang out.

"All right, all right, I'm coming," Chris called back with a smile. "I'll be there in a second!"

He was wrapping up an e-mail, about to head down the hall, when the sound of barking reached his ears.

Without taking his eyes off the screen, Chris wondered, *What are those three dogs up to now?*

Chris Duke had always been a dog person.

Growing up on a farm in Georgia, he'd been surrounded by the lovable, loyal creatures. His family raised greyhounds that raced on dog tracks across the United States. When the dogs retired, they returned to Georgia where the Dukes would find good homes for them. At one point there were about fifty greyhounds on the property.

So when one of Chris's lieutenants picked up a stray puppy on his way to the base in Dand Patan, Chris had been excited. The lieutenant had named the tan and white ball of fur Sasha. Sasha liked nothing more than being around the soldiers. She was always underfoot and they had to be careful not to trip over her. But Chris was glad to have the pup for company.

Each day, as Chris and the other soldiers left the base to visit with Afghan commanders or go on patrol duty, Sasha would happily pad after them — until they crossed the two-foot-deep drainage ditch that surrounded the base.

Sasha was still too small to jump over it. The first few times she'd tried sent her tumbling into the ditch. Chris had to go back, scoop her up, and put her back on the base side of the ditch, where she would whimper and cry to come along.

"You'll be safer here," Chris soothed.

Not everyone on the base shared Chris's love of dogs — and he supposed they had good reason. Packs of wild dogs often swept through the compound, raising a ruckus and leaving a path of torn-up garbage and dug-up waste in their wake.

Sasha cowered from all of the other strays — except for one: a yellow dog with a black snout.

This larger, older female had a slight limp, and Chris knew she'd been shot at some point. Another soldier told Chris that someone had thrown rocks at her. She'd even been run over by a pickup truck. But in spite of all this abuse, she became a kind of mother to Sasha.

"She's part of our pack now," Chris said to one of his roommates as they watched the two dogs sleeping side by side in the shade.

"She can stay here. Hopefully, we can protect her from being such a target."

The yellow dog's head swiveled around. She looked at Chris, with her tail thumping the dusty ground.

"I think she likes the name," Chris said. "Come here, Target."

The newly named Target trotted over to him and Chris nuzzled her face. Not one to miss out when affection was being doled out, Sasha quickly bounded over to join them.

Rufus was the last dog to join the "three mutt-keteers." Chris couldn't remember exactly when he arrived. The collie mix looked to be about two years old, and had simply appeared in the compound one day. Sasha and Target were still fearful of other strays, but they warmed up to Rufus right away.

Whenever Chris would toss a ball or stick for Rufus to fetch, the dog would just look at him for a second. Then he'd put his paws out in front of him, as if to say, "I've got a better idea. Let's wrestle!"

None of the three dogs really liked to chase toys, but they all loved to roughhouse. Chris would get down on the ground and roll around with his pals.

Chris was in a strange place in a faraway country. But he loved having the familiar feel of dog fur under his hands and a friendly lick or a wagging tail greet him when he got back to base after a long, dusty mission. The dogs were always there, waiting for him and the other returning soldiers. Their rambunctious antics never failed to make him feel less homesick.

Chris would have let the dogs sleep inside the barracks at night, but of course that was against regulations. So Sasha, Target, and Rufus normally slept right outside the door of the barracks or across the small road at the base's tactical operations center, or TOC. And once they curled up to sleep, they were usually quiet all night.

But not tonight.

"Sasha! Target! Rufus!" Ryan shouted as the dogs continued to bark. "Come on, guys, knock it off! We're trying to watch a movie!"

"Chris!" Scott called. "Get them to quiet down, would you?"

"Just a second," Chris said. He'd almost finished his e-mail.

Then out of the corner of his eye, Chris saw that a man in everyday Afghan clothes was opening the door to the barracks. That wasn't uncommon, of course. Afghan civilians walked through the building all the time.

But Chris's normally friendly dogs were behaving really oddly. Their barking had reached a fever pitch and their frantic bodies were a blur of motion as they surrounded the man.

The bomber had opened the door to the barracks, and was about to take a step inside, when the three barking dogs leapt on him. The teeth of one sank into his arm and pulled him back. Another dog darted between the bomber's body and the door. The third bit his leg.

The man shouted and struggled against them. But the dogs wouldn't let go.

How do they know what I'm planning to do?

The bomber had no choice. This was not the way he'd wanted things to go.

He reached for the detonator again.

And this time he pressed it.

Ka-BLAM!

The world rushed at Chris. And time seemed to slow down — something that looked like a giant fifty-caliber bullet whizzed past his head. What he thought was a door blew past him.

The explosion threw Chris out of his chair. He flew backward across the hallway and skittered along the floor of another soldier's room.

The soldier inside looked up from his bed, shock apparent on his face. "What — ?"

Moving automatically, Chris popped back up to his feet and raced out of the room.

What was that chemical smell? He struggled to understand what was happening. Oh right, there had been an explosion!

He was dazed, but his body had kicked into survival mode. He needed to keep moving, to get his vest and helmet on in case any more bombs were detonated.

Before he could, something warm spread across the left side of his chest.

I'm bleeding, he thought in a hazy way. *I'm hurt. I should really see a medic. . . .*

He walked into another room. "I need help, Doc," he said and then realized he was actually standing in front of three privates — not medics. The privates reached for Chris. Their mouths moved but Chris couldn't hear them over the ringing in his ears.

"You can't help me," Chris said simply and walked back out of the room.

By now, black smoke filled the hallway. The explosion had knocked out the overhead light, so half of the hallway was pitch-black. Buddies called out to one another and medics shouted orders.

Chris made his way through the controlled chaos to the medics' quarters as his hearing began to return.

Worried about the damage he might see, Chris didn't dare look down at his wounded chest. He just lifted his shirt and waited for one of the medics to give him the bad news.

"You're going to be all right, Chris," the medic said. "You've got a puncture wound that's only about as big as your little finger."

He gave Chris a bandage so he could clean and dress his own wound. That was all Chris needed for his brain to clear, and for a coherent thought — the first since the explosion — to pop into his head.

Are Scott and Ryan okay?

Chris ran to his room. The bomb had exploded just outside the building, on the other side of the front door. The force had killed the bomber and blown a hole the size of a softball in the wall right over Ryan's cot. *Exactly where he leans when he plays* Call of Duty, Chris thought.

Ryan was wounded, and shrapnel covered his back. But if he'd still been sitting there playing the game, he would not have survived.

His friend was clearly stunned. "I moved a split second before the explosion," he told Chris.

The door to their room had blown off its hinges and slammed down on top of Sergeant Conrad Porter's bed. He was on leave this week, otherwise he would have been crushed.

Still, Chris could see things would have been much worse if the bomb had gone off inside the barracks instead of outside. They would all be dead.

"Scott, you all right?" Chris asked.

Scott looked down at the cuts on his arms and legs. "I think so," he said. "The dogs . . . that's why they were going crazy. They saw the bomber."

Flashes of the memory shot through Chris's brain like lightning. He saw the man opening the door, saw the dogs jumping on him —

The dogs!

Chris turned to go check on Rufus, Sasha, and Target. A medic rushed into the room and shoved a 9mm pistol in Chris's hand.

"Hang on," Chris said. "I just need to find the dogs to —"

"Let's move, Sergeant. Now," the medic said. "We're locking down the base, and we're getting you on a helicopter to the trauma center in Sharana."

The medic and another soldier with an M-4 rifle led Chris back down the hall and out the side exit of the barracks. The cool night air was filled with the sounds of shouting and rushing feet as the compound was secured.

With his two roommates close behind, Chris was pulled across the small access road to the TOC where the army had set up a small aid station.

The medic grabbed the radio and called for a helicopter. Chris craned his neck to look out the TOC's window. From this angle, he couldn't see the front of the barracks or what might have happened to the dogs. And Scott and Ryan hadn't seen any sign of them on their way over to the TOC.

"I saw them," the medic said when he got off the radio. "While I was running over to the barracks after the explosion, I saw the dogs scurrying off."

"All three of them?" Chris asked.

The medic nodded. "They're all hurt, one more than the others."

As the sounds of an approaching helicopter filled the air, Chris asked for more details, but the medic shook his head. "That's all I know. There was too much going on and I was worried about human casualties. It's incredible that no one was killed."

For the four days he was at the trauma center in Sharana, Chris tried to get information about the dogs. But either no one knew anything — or they didn't want to tell Chris the truth and upset him.

So when the helicopter brought Chris, Ryan, and Scott back to the base in Dand Patan, the dogs were the first thing on Chris's mind. As the helicopter landed, they were met by their fourth roommate, Conrad, who'd returned from leave.

"Where's Rufus?" Chris asked after they'd all greeted one another with hugs. "Where are the dogs?"

Not waiting for an answer, Chris rushed back to the main compound.

"Chris," Conrad said, following after him. "Hold on a second."

But Chris had been waiting for four days. He didn't want to wait any longer to see the dogs. As he scanned the base for any sign of them, he saw the damage the bomb had done. It had ripped the front door off the barracks, leaving a huge hole that was now covered with tarps. If the dogs had been anywhere near the door during the explosion, they might be hurt beyond help.

Conrad caught up with Chris, and pulled him over to the side of the mess hall next to a large wooden crate.

"Where are they?" Chris demanded.

"Sasha . . ." Conrad didn't seem able to finish.

"What?" Chris felt something in his heart crack. He knew what was coming.

Conrad took a breath. "We found Sasha the day after the attack. Her wounds were too bad, buddy. We had to put her down. I'm sorry."

Chris couldn't believe it. Sasha — that cute, bumbling ball of fur — was dead.

"Rufus? What about Target? Is she gone, too?"

Before Conrad could answer, a yellow head popped out of the crate next to them.

"Target!" Chris shouted.

Wagging her tail, she carried something in her mouth and stepped closer to Chris. She moved slowly as if she didn't want to get too far from the box. She put the squirming creature at his feet. It was a tiny, pink puppy. Chris hunkered down next to them.

"Target was in rough shape after the bomb went off," Conrad explained. "The medic barely saved her life. She went into early labor."

"She was pregnant?" Chris said, surprised. None of them had known!

"That's right," Conrad said. "She had five puppies. Or at least we think she did. She hasn't let anyone get too close to them." Then he added with a smile, "Until now."

Target lifted her head so Chris could scratch under her chin. Her fur was matted and she had small cuts all over.

"And Rufus?" Chris barely dared to ask. "Is he okay? Just tell me."

Conrad pointed behind Chris, who looked over his shoulder. There was his friend Rufus. With a limp, the dog was meandering toward the front gates, looking a little lost. Before Chris could say anything, Rufus lifted his nose to the air. He turned his head and his eyes locked on Chris's.

The dog hobbled over to them. A bandage on his back covered a wound the size of a silver dollar.

"He may seem a little out of it," Conrad said. "No one's been too sure how to treat his wounds. So we've been keeping him pretty sedated."

Chris gently hugged the dog's neck. "Wow, Rufus," he said. "Am I glad to see you."

After visiting the spot near the compound where Sasha had been buried, Chris focused all of his attention on Target, her puppies, and making sure that Rufus got better. When he and one of the base medics removed the makeshift bandage from Rufus's back, Chris could actually see the wall of the dog's stomach and a few of his other organs.

"If we don't get more help," the medic said, "I'm not sure if Rufus is going to make it."

It took a couple of tries but they were able to get the top army veterinarian on the phone.

"I can't spend my time helping stray dogs," the veterinarian snapped. "We have enough animals — like horses and bomb-sniffing dogs — that are officially part of the army to treat."

"It's just . . ." Chris trailed off. He wasn't sure how to put everything into words. How could he quickly explain that this dog had saved his life? That this dog deserved their help?

Something in the pause must have connected with the veterinarian.

"But who knows how the cyber world works, right?" she said, her voice more gentle now. "You might *accidentally* get an unauthorized e-mail with instructions on how to care for Rufus's wound."

"That would be amazing," Chris said.

"And the next chopper from Sharana might *accidentally* bring some medicine to help Rufus."

"Thanks, Doctor."

"For what?" she said with a small chuckle. "Accidents happen."

During the remainder of his stay in Afghanistan, Chris was no longer sent off the base. Instead, he pulled guard duty each night — and each day he spent with Rufus.

Every twenty-four hours, he took Rufus to the TOC's aid station and repacked his wound, pulling the gauze out, cleaning the puncture, and repacking it with fresh gauze — all as the army vet had instructed in her e-mail. He slowly nursed Rufus back to health, but he knew that his time with the pup was coming to an end.

Chris and his unit had been in Afghanistan for eight months. In a few weeks, they would be deployed back to the United States. He would be leaving, and he wanted to take Rufus, Target, and her puppies with him.

"We can't leave them here," Chris said to his roommates. "If we can chip in for the cost of transporting them, I bet we can bring them back home."

They all agreed, and began asking others in the unit for donations of five or ten dollars.

"Five bucks?" one soldier asked. "To help those dogs? No way." Then he fished into his pocket for his wallet. "Let's make it twenty."

We can do this, Chris thought. *We can get them out of Afghanistan.*

He was sitting down, rubbing Rufus's belly outside the barracks, when Conrad walked out of the base commander's office and joined him. Conrad's face was grim.

"I just had a meeting with the higher-ups," he said, kicking the dust at his feet. "They said no to our plan. The dogs can't leave Afghanistan."

"Why?" Chris said, jumping to his feet. "The dogs won't be safe!"

"I know," Conrad agreed. "But the army says if they let us help these dogs, it will never end. They'll have to let everyone help every stray around. It will be overwhelming."

"But these dogs are the ones that helped us!" Chris said, his voice rising angrily. "They saved us first. We owe them!"

Conrad just shook his head. "I know, buddy, I'm sorry. The dogs will have to stay here."

Chris's gear was all packed. The choppers waited to take him and the other Guardsmen off the base to begin their journey back to the United States. There was just one more thing to do, something he'd been putting off as long as possible. He had to say good-bye to the dogs.

"Don't worry, Chris," Scott said. "The Vermont National Guard is coming here next. Those guys will watch out for the dogs."

Chris didn't doubt there were good people in the incoming unit. He knew they would try to help the dogs. But things were so unpredictable in Afghanistan. What if the unit got moved again, and the dogs didn't make the trip? It wouldn't be anyone's fault, but the dogs would be left to fend for themselves.

Crouching down, Chris called to Target and Rufus. They trotted over and he patted each dog on the head. Then he stood up.

"That's it, Chris?" Ryan asked.

Chris nodded. He couldn't speak. Saying good-bye to Target and Rufus was even tougher than he'd thought it would be. Like the pieces of shrapnel still in his chest, they would always be a part of him.

But he didn't want to draw things out and upset the dogs. He wanted to leave them with positive feelings for him.

Trying to keep it together, Chris picked up his bag and headed for the helicopter.

"Chris, are you okay?" Lauren, his wife, asked as they left the gym together after a workout. "You seem like your brain is miles away."

"Sorry," he said. "Just thinking about the dogs."

Chris had been home in Georgia for three weeks. But he couldn't help worrying about Rufus and Target. He was safe in the United States while the dogs that had saved his life were stuck in Afghanistan.

And new worries had crept into his mind. What if the incoming unit didn't know how to take care of the dogs? Or what if the unit leaders followed strict army policy and ran the dogs off the compound? They'd have to fight for every tiny scrap of food. With his injuries, Rufus would never survive. And how would Target feed her puppies?

When Chris and Lauren walked into their house that afternoon, the phone was ringing.

"Hi," a woman said when Chris picked up the phone. "My name is Francis Esposito. My fiancé is Specialist Douglas Gruber. He's been caring for Rufus and Target. He told me about what the dogs did. They're heroes and they deserve to be here. I want to help you bring the dogs to the United States."

"How?" Chris asked uncertainly. He'd tried many times since he'd gotten home. Each attempt had led to nothing but heartbreak. He'd been told again and again by the military higher-ups to forget about it.

But Francis had a plan. She created a website to help. Over the next few months, news spread across the country and around the world about the mission to get the brave dogs out of Afghanistan. Soon people from all walks of life joined the fight to give them a new home.

On the morning of July 29, 2010, Chris and his wife arrived at the DeKalb Peachtree Airport in Georgia to meet a plane.

Newspaper and television camera crews surrounded them as Chris and Lauren waited anxiously in baggage claim. Volunteers who had given their time to make this day happen chatted quietly around them.

Then a hush fell over the room as the sounds of clicking paws on the tiled floor approached. Slowly Rufus and Target walked around the corner.

Rufus spotted Chris immediately. It had been a long trip from Afghanistan, with a stopover in New York City, but Rufus's tail started wagging like crazy. He hurried over as Chris reached out to touch him.

Up until this very second, Chris had not let himself believe that he would ever see either of the dogs again. And now here they were.

"Hey, buddy," Chris whispered, stroking Rufus's back. He felt the wound there. But it was healing nicely.

"Are you okay, buddy?" Chris asked. He crouched down to get closer to his friend. "Are you scared? You want to lie down?"

As an answer, Rufus plopped onto the floor and let Chris rub his belly. Target hurried over to them, and Chris reached out to pet her, too.

One of the reporters called out, "The dogs wouldn't be here in the United States if it wasn't for you, Chris."

"Well, I wouldn't be here, either, if it wasn't for them," Chris replied. And then he turned his attention back to Rufus and Target. "You're home."

A few minutes later, Chris and Lauren walked out of the terminal with Target on one side and Rufus on the other. They were ready to start their new lives together.

Chris finished his National Guard active duty contract and now works as a fireman. Rufus lives with Chris, his wife, and three other dogs on their wooded property where he can wander and play. Target stayed with them for a couple of weeks, before they sent her to live in Arizona with the medic who had saved her life in Afghanistan. The Dukes had bonded with Target, so it was hard for them to say good-bye to her. Target's five puppies were also brought over to a new home in the United States.

A SECOND TO SAVE

WHEN EVERY MOMENT COUNTS, A RESCUE COMBAT FLIGHT MEDIC RISKS IT ALL TO SAVE THOSE WOUNDED IN BATTLE

Air Force Tech Sergeant Mark DeCorte sat in the open door of the soaring Pave Hawk helicopter, his legs dangling outside. The enemy territory below glowed green through his night vision goggles.

It was the summer of 2006, and Mark was flying on a mission two hours outside of Kandahar in Afghanistan. His Pave Hawk and an Apache helicopter were serving as gunships, guarding three giant two-rotor choppers called Chinooks. The Chinooks carried supplies urgently needed by U.S. troops fighting the Taliban.

As the radio crackled over Mark's headset, he scanned the dark desert landscape, searching for Taliban rockets. If he spotted one, he'd shout "Break right!" or "Break left!"

The pilot knew to respond instantly. Their lives depended on dodging those rockets quickly.

It was something other than a rocket that caught Mark's eye, though. His attention snapped to the Apache helicopter about a half a football field away. The chopper swung toward the Pave Hawk and then dodged away. Then it swung back toward them —

And it kept coming. The gap between the two helicopters swiftly closed.

Mark waited a heartbeat for the Apache to swing the other way. But it just continued on its course toward the Pave Hawk, faster and faster.

What's that pilot doing? He must not see us!

Mark pushed his mic button. He sucked in a breath and was about to yell —

"Break right!" the gunner behind him shouted, beating Mark to the punch. He grabbed Mark's belt to hold him steady. Good thing. Mark was tossed forward — and nearly out the door — as the Pave Hawk jerked right.

Before soaring apart, the two helicopters came so close that Mark could read the small writing on the side of the Apache.

"Thanks," Mark told the gunner, his mind still buzzing as the Pave Hawk leveled out and the Apache resumed its normal course. But Mark barely had time to get his balance when —

"Mayday, mayday!" a voice yelled over the radio. It was the pilot of one of the Chinooks below. "Mayday! Aircraft in distress!"

The Chinook's hydraulic lines had ruptured, crippling the aircraft. Had it been hit by enemy fire from Taliban forces on the ground? The Chinook was going in hot for a hard landing.

A confusion of voices erupted from the radio: "— fluid — it's in — eyes!"

Mark and the four other men on his crew pieced the situation together. Hydraulic fluid had sprayed into the eyes of the Chinook's flight engineer. The FE was the soldier in charge of watching over the chopper's systems and the cargo. That fluid burned human tissue and needed to be flushed out fast — or the FE could go blind.

As the Chinook fell to the ground, disappearing in a cloud of desert dust, Mark's pilot turned and asked him, "Do you think you can help that FE?"

Mark answered without hesitation. "Get me down there," he said, throwing on his medical pack. "Let's do it."

✴

Mark was part of a new military "experiment."

In 2005, army flight medics were spread thin across Iraq and Afghanistan. The army wanted to find a way to reach wounded soldiers faster and save more lives.

To help, the air force asked Mark and two other medics to fly with different teams directly into combat situations. This was a huge change.

Usually, wounded soldiers had to wait for an area to be cleared and the action to subside before a MEDEVAC, or rescue helicopter, could safely land. As a combat rescue flight medic, Mark entered active combat zones — with battles raging all around him — to provide urgent care quickly.

Mark paid a price for this opportunity. Under the Geneva Conventions, medics were not supposed to be fired upon by the enemy. But because Mark was now in the heat of the action, he was considered a combatant — and therefore a target.

If Mark ever needed encouragement, he just thought of the tan footprints painted on the side-sliding door of his Pave Hawk. Each footprint represented a "save" — a life that would have been lost if not for Mark and the other medics on board.

And Mark planned on adding to that record tonight.

✳

The Chinook's rotors — and now the Pave Hawk's — stirred up desert dust one hundred fifty feet in all directions as they came in for a landing. The resulting brownout meant they couldn't see a thing and forced the pilot to rely on the craft's instruments to land.

As always, Mark was ready to jump from the chopper the instant it touched down. He had a standing order to stay tethered to the Pave Hawk. That way, the pilot could take off immediately in the event of an attack and Mark would be pulled up with the helicopter. But the wounded were often well beyond the landing zone. The only way to get to them was to leave the rotor area. So even though Mark wasn't sure where enemy forces might be hiding, he unclipped from the helicopter and ran into the darkness toward the Chinook.

If the Pave Hawk had to take off, Mark would be left behind.

But the risk was worth the reward. Mark was here to help people. He knew the crew of the Chinook had no way of treating the wounded FE. Every second counted as the fluid burned the man's eyes.

The Chinook's ramp was down. The crew must have lowered it as they landed. Mark sprinted up into the craft.

Where's the wounded man? There!

Mark pulled the flight engineer outside and laid him on the ground. Popping open his landing-zone bag, Mark took out two bags of IV fluid and cut the corners. He poured a bag into each of the FE's eyes at the same time to flush them out.

I don't have enough.

The rest of the fluid and other equipment were back in Mark's copter. Mark got the FE to his feet and half carried him to the Pave

Hawk. Once they reached Mark's tiny work space in the back, he broke open a nasal cannula — a device that sprayed oxygen up a patient's nose. Mark needed it to do something different tonight.

"Hold this between your eyes," Mark told the FE. He attached the nasal cannula to another IV bag. Now it constantly flushed fluid into the FE's eyes.

"Ah, man, man," the flight engineer moaned in pain.

The Pave Hawk lifted into the air, starting the long trip back to Kandahar. All the way, as he continued to treat the wounded man, Mark wondered . . .

Was the FE's career over? Was his life about to change forever? *Will he go blind?*

The next evening, just after midnight, Mark and his crew were called to their base's tactical operations center.

"One of our squads is pinned down in a ravine, taking Taliban fire from two positions," said the commanding officer, or CO, as he pointed at a satellite photo. "Our forces are out of water, nearly out of ammo, and two of their M-240 machine guns have seized up from overfiring. We need to resupply them." Here the CO paused, and then asked, "What will it be, men?"

Mark and the four members of his crew shared a look.

They could speak up if they thought the mission was too dangerous. But after months together, they knew one another and how an operation like this would work.

While the rest of the crew rushed to the copter to load supplies and turn rotors, Mark and the pilot, Nick, stayed behind, gathering more intelligence to build their situational awareness, or SA. This was vital for a successful mission — and for survival.

Minutes later, Mark headed through the outer offices to join his crew. As he rounded a corner, he overheard someone reading letters from an eye chart on an exam room wall. "H, O, N, S, C, V."

It was the wounded FE from the night before. The flight doc who was examining him gazed into his eyes, and then stepped back. "Soldier," she told the FE, sounding amazed, "you're cleared to fly." Mark's quick intervention had saved his eyesight.

The FE rushed past Mark with a nod, clearly not recognizing him.

Mark poked his head in the exam room to talk with the flight doc. "Hey, Emilee, you're returning that FE to flying status a day after the accident?"

"The day after? No," the flight doc said, shaking her head. "I was just rechecking him. He went back out last night after you brought him in. His eyes had zero damage."

Mark grinned as he headed out to the chopper.

It was a three-hour flight to the squad that was under attack by the Taliban. Mark took his spot in the chopper, sitting in the open doorway in the back. The air grew colder as they climbed high over the mountainous terrain.

"Uh, do you guys see that?" asked Mike, the FE.

Mark looked toward the front of the chopper. Even in the near pitch-black sky, it was hard to miss the side of a mountain rushing toward them like a wall. The Pave Hawk's powerful engines climbed and climbed, struggling to get over the top of the mountain. The chopper's blades were trying to catch on the thin air of the high altitude, but it looked like they weren't going to make it!

Nick jerked the controls and the helicopter banked sharply, turning all the way around.

"Sorry, guys," he said as Mark and the others were thrown about. "Let's try that again."

Nick circled the Pave Hawk around and took another run at the mountaintop. This time he came in faster — and lower — using the air current for a little extra lift.

"Here we go!" Mark said to himself.

It was a white-knuckle ride. Like a roller coaster cresting a peak, the Pave Hawk rose on a rush of air.

This time they made it over the top of the mountain.

Forty minutes later, the Pave Hawk flew over the battle area. Thirteen soldiers were stuck in a ravine. Taliban forces had them surrounded and fired down on them from the hillside above.

On board the Pave Hawk, it was time for a gut check. This was another chance for the crew to call off the mission. Any of them could tell the pilot, "No, this is too risky."

After all, who would fly into a firefight?

I would, Mark thought.

"Our guys are in trouble down there," Mark said into his headset.

"Agreed," Mike said. "But where are we supposed to land?"

Nick and the copilot, Chris, peered down into the darkness. The only likely landing zone was a small space on a hill between large rocks and scrubby trees. Dropping into that tight box would be tricky — but taking off could be even more difficult. If the Pave Hawk was attacked before the crew had a chance to unload the ammo, water, and guns for the stranded soldiers, it might be too heavy to get away safely.

The chopper might have to hover, turn one hundred eighty degrees, and go out the way it had arrived. By that time, the enemy would know exactly where to fire as the helicopter took off.

It was a chance the crew was willing to take. They all gave the thumbs-up.

"We're a go," Mark said. As the copter plunged down, his adrenaline fired into overdrive and he grabbed his medical pack.

He positioned himself to leap off the Pave Hawk. He had one hand on his belt, ready to unclip from the tether. They needed to get the supplies to the men and get out of there before they were attacked themselves.

The chopper descended into the brownout. At the last second, Mark could see the slanted ground racing up toward them fast —

Wham!

The Pave Hawk came down hard. Too hard.

Mark was thrown through the door. His tether extended, jerking him to a stop as he slammed into the rocky mountainside.

Thank God I hadn't unclipped yet, he thought.

If the pilot lifted off, Mark would be pulled up, too. That was the good news.

But there was also bad news. The Pave Hawk was rolling

backward downhill. And Mark was in its path. A wheel was about to crush his legs!

Mark couldn't roll out of the way because he was still tethered to the chopper. He started crabbing backward, his heavy gear slowing him down.

The wheel rolled closer. Mark scrambled back. They continued this race for two feet...ten feet...fifteen feet until the Pave Hawk finally came to a rest.

Oh man. That was close!

He jumped to his feet, untethered himself, and hopped back into the chopper. They had to unload the supplies fast. He grabbed one of the bags and jerked it toward the door. It didn't move. He bore down and pulled as hard as he could. Still nothing. The bag wouldn't budge.

Of course!

Each of the three bags was stuffed to capacity. Mark had actually used body bags to store the supplies because they were the biggest, strongest bags available. One was filled with five-gallon water containers, one with a bunch of ammunition, and the third with two M-240 machine guns. It had taken five people to load them all.

"I'll give you a hand," offered Ben, the gunner.

No, Ben! Don't leave your gun! Mark wanted to shout. But then he realized he needed help if they were going to get out of this ravine anytime soon. The Taliban could be heading toward them this very second.

Ben untethered from the Pave Hawk. Mark and the gunner would be stranded if they were attacked and the Pave Hawk had to take off.

And they wouldn't be alone. Mike had also unclipped to check out the damage to the helicopter. The FE was off weapon, walking around the aircraft to make sure they could take off.

With no one weapon-ready, they were defenseless. They couldn't even talk to the pilot when they were disconnected from their radios.

It's all for the greater good, Mark reminded himself as he and the gunner dragged the bags off the Pave Hawk and onto the dusty ground.

He focused on the task at hand, blocking out thoughts of Taliban soldiers who must be swarming in the darkness all around them.

"Wow, I'm glad to see you guys," said the young squad leader, as Mark and his gunner handed over the bags.

Knowing that Taliban forces on the surrounding hills might be training their gun sights on them, Mark and his gunner had practically crawled from the Pave Hawk to the ravine. They had pulled the heavy bags a short distance, one at a time. They kept moving in short spurts until they finally reached the exhausted squad.

The U.S. soldiers had been fighting a long battle made worse without water and with a dwindling store of ammo. The supplies Mark's crew delivered were sorely needed.

The squad leader signed a receipt, showing he'd received the delivery.

Mark couldn't help laughing as he took the receipt and tucked it in his pocket. "In the middle of all this, we're doing paperwork."

The squad leader chuckled, his tired eyes crinkling with a smile. "Good luck on the trip back."

Keeping their heads down, Mark and Ben hurried back to the helicopter. Just as they reached the left door, Mike came around from the other side. He'd just finished his inspection of the Pave Hawk.

Mike gave Mark a shrug that said it all. The copter had been damaged in the hard landing, but what choice did they have? They had to try to get out of there.

With that less than ringing endorsement, the men climbed on board.

Once they were all tethered and connected to the radio again, Mark said, "We're good to go."

"Let's just hope the chopper is," Ben added.

Mark's eyes darted to the flight control panel, and he felt a sinking in his stomach. Gauges that were normally lit up were black.

That's not a good sign.

"Fingers crossed, men," the pilot said, flicking switches.

In an instant, the engines roared to full power. Ben hooted in excitement. They were just seconds away from takeoff!

"Get ready for a bumpy ride," Chris warned from the copilot seat as the rotors started turning faster.

Then a call came over the radio. Right after Mark and Ben had left, the squad had captured an injured Taliban fighter. He was unconscious and would die without medical treatment. Two U.S. soldiers were carrying him toward the helicopter now.

Did Mark and his crew want to wait in this danger zone to save the enemy?

For a split second, Mark's mind went back a month earlier. He and his crew were operating near a forward surgical team (FST) when a call came in from a small village.

"A nine-year-old Afghan has lost his hand," the report said. "A rocket-propelled grenade he was holding exploded. He won't live longer than twenty minutes without medical help."

"Oh man," Nick said. "It will take five minutes to get to the copter and get it running. And the flight time is about fifteen minutes."

"That's twenty minutes right there," Chris said. "What are we going to do?"

"Get moving," Mark said.

And that was what they did. Somehow they'd reached the village in record time, and Mark was "feet down" inside of twenty minutes. He'd lifted the nine-year-old Afghan boy in his arms and they were back in the air in an instant.

The boy's wound was bad and required the equipment and personnel of a hospital. There wasn't much Mark could do for a traumatic injury like this on the Pave Hawk. Just stop the bleeding with tourniquets and administer IVs, oxygen, bandages, and a blanket . . . and comfort the boy, who shied away from Mark's touch at first.

The boy had probably never been on an aircraft. His wound, the noise of the machinery, being surrounded by Americans he didn't know — everything must have been very frightening.

To see if he could ease the boy's fears, Mark dug out a stuffed animal he kept in his kit. The boy pulled the toy to his chest with his good arm. Mark looked into the scared child's eyes and hugged him.

With that hug, Mark felt something in the boy change. The boy hugged him back.

As the Pave Hawk raced back to the FST in record time, Mark and his crew weren't thinking about whether or not the boy considered them an enemy. They were thinking about saving his life — which they did.

Mark knew that many soldiers would look at an injured Taliban fighter, like the one his crew was being called to help, as the enemy. Others might see a source of intelligence.

How did Mark see him?

As a patient.

"Hold on!" Mark said. "I'm going back out for that guy!"

Before his crew could respond, Mark untethered and jumped out of the helicopter. He dashed under the spinning blades and across the short distance to where two U.S. soldiers stood over the wounded Taliban fighter.

Mark quickly examined the unconscious man. He'd been shot in both legs and was losing a lot of blood. He was going into shock and would be dead soon if Mark didn't do something.

Moving fast, Mark pulled two tourniquets from around his ankles — he kept them there for easy access — and tied them around the man's legs.

The pain of the pressure brought the man back to consciousness. He came out of his daze swinging. Yelling in his native Dari tongue, the combative man started punching Mark, who struggled to avoid the man's blows.

"We've got to go," the FE signaled with a wave from the helicopter. "Now!"

Mark dragged the wounded man by the shoulders and, ducking under the turning rotors, got him on the chopper. Just as he climbed on board, the helicopter lurched upward.

The patient was now fighting Mark with everything he had. Lashing out, punching, scratching.

No hugs or toys are going to soothe him.

Glancing at the open door, Mark thought, *He could push me out!*

The helicopter was bucking slightly. They had dropped a lot of weight with the supplies, but was it enough to get them out of the small landing area? And, after the hard landing, could the Pave Hawk make the long trip back to Kandahar?

Meanwhile, the patient kept fighting Mark tooth and nail. Mark knew the man must be panicking. But he had to get an IV and pain medication into the patient. And he had only one hand to do it. The other was busy blocking the man's fists and trying to hold him down.

It was going to be a long flight back to the base.

Mark lay sprawled on top of the patient, restraining him and keeping him from hurting himself or the crew.

As he glanced out the Pave Hawk's window, his heart leapt at the orange glow of landing lights in the distance.

Kandahar.

Relief washed over him. "We're going to make it!"

He actually started to laugh as his morale soared. Mark felt like a World War II bomber returning home after a long mission. No one in the crew had been hurt tonight. They had helped thirteen men survive a battle. And they had saved a wounded man.

Now that their trip was ending, Mark and the rest of the crew suddenly grew quiet. It had been a wild roller coaster of a mission. Yet they'd done good work.

The patient continued to struggle, but Mark restrained him and made sure his IV was still in place.

"You may not like me now," Mark told his patient, not sure if the man could understand him. "But when we're both older, you may feel differently."

Helping bring wounded Taliban fighters back to full health was important. Mark knew that when the man was eventually released and returned home, he would tell his family about the good things Mark and his crew had done for him.

Maybe that's the biggest effect I can have here, Mark thought.

The Pave Hawk touched down on the base's landing pad. The pilot had radioed ahead, and a medical crew was waiting to rush the wounded man into the operating room. As the rotors started to power down, Mark stepped off the chopper and sighed at the feel of solid ground beneath his feet.

He helped two base medics unload the wounded man. One of the medics gave Mark a questioning look, as if to ask, "Is he going to make it?"

As an answer, Mark pointed to the tan footprints on the side of the Pave Hawk.

They could add one more.

While stationed in Kandahar, Mark DeCorte flew on sixty-three combat rescue missions and saved thirty-six lives, while also resupplying coalition forces. Several of these missions have been combined in this telling, and names and locations have been changed to ensure operational security. In addition to being promoted to senior master sergeant, Mark received awards and decorations that include three Air Medals, the Aerial Achievement Medal, four Commendation Medals, the Joint Service Achievement Medal, seven Air Force Achievement Medals, and the Air Force Combat Action Medal. The successful creation of combat rescue flight medics contributed to a first in history: an increase in the survivability rate of battlefield casualties to 90 percent.

CAUGHT IN THE CROSSFIRE

FIFTY BOYS AND THEIR TEACHERS ARE TRAPPED IN AN ORPHANAGE AS A BATTLE
BETWEEN THE TALIBAN AND THE PAKISTANI MILITARY RAGES AROUND THEM

"Wake up!"

Early on the morning of May 6, 2009, sixteen-year-old Hameed Malam struggled up out of a deep sleep. One of his teachers at the orphanage in Pakistan's Swat Valley was shaking him awake.

"What's the matter?" Hameed sat up. He couldn't see a thing in the dark room. Then he squinted as lightning flashed and thunder boomed outside.

The teacher, Omar Khan, darted around the room, making sure each of the twenty boys who slept in the room was awake.

Hameed reached for the light switch.

"No! Leave the light off!" Omar shouted, surprising all the boys. The teacher never raised his voice. "We must get downstairs," he said urgently. "Come."

Outside the window, lightning lit up the sky again. The glass panes rattled — and one cracked.

Hameed gasped. That wasn't lightning. That was an explosion.

Then another! And each blast sounded closer to the building than the one before.

It's all starting again, Hameed thought. *The attacks, the bombs.*

"Let's go, boys!" Omar said, hustling the other boys out of the room toward the staircase. Hameed dashed the other way down the hall.

"Where are you going, Hameed?" Omar shouted. "I've been to the younger boys' room already. They're all downstairs!"

Not all of them. Not if Hameed knew his little brother.

He rushed into the darkness of the younger boys' room, which looked empty.

Ker-BLAK! Ker-BLAK!

Two mortar shells exploded, one after another, out on the street. The walls of the room shook and plaster crumbled from the ceiling. In the flashes of light, Hameed saw a familiar brown blanket bunched in the far corner of the room. Rushing over, he lifted up one end of the blanket.

His seven-year-old brother, Anas, trembled underneath. This was where he always hid when he was scared. Anas blinked up at Hameed with wide eyes. "Hameed, what's happening?"

Hameed didn't want to tell Anas the truth: that the Taliban was attacking their neighborhood, and the Pakistani government soldiers stationed upstairs were firing back.

Two weeks ago, Pakistani soldiers had built sandbag bunkers on the roof and on the top floor of the four-story orphanage to use as a lookout.

Hameed needed to get Anas downstairs, not scare him more. So he didn't say any of that. Instead, he leaned down to pick him up.

Anas pushed back. "No, don't lift me up. I'm big now. I can walk on my own."

This wasn't the time to fight. Hameed took Anas's arm and pulled him quickly out the door. They had to get downstairs, away from the windows.

Halfway down the hall, Anas suddenly stopped and struggled to go back. "My blanket! I forgot my blanket."

Gunfire filled the night. Hameed knew the Taliban must be very close now.

"You're big now, remember?" Hameed said, tugging him along. "You can do without the blanket for a night. We'll get it tomorrow...."

If the building is still standing, he added silently.

The storeroom at the back of the Mingora Orphanage for Boys had no windows and was slightly underground, making it the safest spot during an attack.

Hameed and Anas had to squeeze inside. Fifty orphans — ranging in age from six to seventeen — and ten adult staff members already cowered there. Many of the boys were crying, scared of what might happen.

Hameed found a place for Anas to sit down. Then he found Mohammad Nawaz, the director of the orphanage. "What's going on, sir?"

"The Taliban have surrounded the orphanage," Mohammad answered in a whisper, not wanting to upset the little ones. "They have rocket launchers and rifles. They say they're shooting at the soldiers on top of the building — not us. But we are under siege. I'm just sorry we couldn't get all of you out in time."

Hameed nodded. In the past few weeks, about one hundred seventy other orphans had been sent to live with distant relatives. The boys who remained here had no family left, not even faraway cousins who could take them in. These were the children who had no one to protect them — like Hameed and his brother, Anas. Their mother and father had been killed when a mortar landed outside their home.

Now as the bombs continued to explode outside the orphanage, Hameed crouched next to three six-year-olds who were sobbing in the far corner. "Let's play *adda kadda*," he suggested, trying to distract them with a version of tic-tac-toe.

"It's too dark," one of the little boys wailed.

"Then you can each say you won, right?" Hameed said with a chuckle. "Who can tell the difference?"

The joke stopped the sobbing for a second, and Hameed was glad for that. They had all been through so much already — and now this latest attack. The very roof over their heads shook. They were on the front lines of a confusing, bloody battle.

As the boys played, Hameed leaned back against a near-empty shelf of rice. Behind him, he could hear Omar and Mohammad talking in hushed tones.

"We have to get the boys out of this city. Mingora is no longer safe," Mohammad was saying. "There's a shelter in Peshawar that could take us in."

"That's over thirty miles away," Omar whispered back. "We can't even get an inch out the front door. There's an around-the-clock curfew. Anyone who goes out during curfew will be shot dead by the soldiers, you know that."

Mohammad nodded gravely. "Then we'll just have to wait."

After two days of nonstop shelling, the streets around the orphanage had become a battleground. The Pakistani soldiers even buried land mines in the orphanage's playground to protect themselves from Taliban attacks.

Trapped inside the small storeroom, the terrified orphans and teachers were running out of food. They had only enough supplies to last one more day.

The power lines had been cut, and Mohammad ran down his cell phone battery calling anyone who might've been able to help.

Desperate, he called a Pakistani TV network that recorded an interview with him. Mohammad begged for the military to leave the orphanage and for the Taliban to stop their attacks. He asked for assistance in getting the boys out, for anyone who was listening to send food. The network ran his story, but no one came to help.

The dark storeroom felt like a prison cell. Everyone was hungry and beginning to go stir-crazy. Rereading a storybook with Anas for what felt like the millionth time, Hameed watched seventeen-year-old Yusuf sneak out the door when none of teachers was watching. Leaving Anas with the book, Hameed followed his friend out to the hall.

"Where are you going?" Hameed whispered. "You can't be out here!"

"I'm stretching my legs," Yusuf said. "I can't stand it in there anymore."

Hameed tried to pull him back to the storeroom, but Yusuf headed for the common area at the front of the orphanage, and Hameed reluctantly followed. They could hear the soldiers moving around upstairs.

Outside the window, Hameed and Yusuf could see a man walking toward the military's main base, just sixty yards from the orphanage. The soldiers were yelling for the man to stop.

Still the man walked on. Something was strapped to his back. . . .

"Get away from the window!" Hameed shouted, pulling Yusuf to the floor as the suicide bomber detonated his explosive. The force ripped across the playground and shattered the front windows of the orphanage.

Glass and plaster sprayed around Yusuf and Hameed. For a moment, they didn't dare move as the gunfire and shouting continued outside. Then Yusuf moaned.

"Are you okay?" Hameed asked. Yusuf nodded slowly. Hameed couldn't believe neither of them had been hurt in the explosion. He helped the still-dazed Yusuf to his feet and led him back toward the storeroom.

"From now on," Hameed said as they hurried along, "when you want to stretch your legs — "

"Don't worry, Hameed," Yusuf interrupted. "No more stretching. Exercise in this place is far too dangerous!"

A day later, Mohammad went up to the roof to plead with the soldiers to leave or to at least help the orphans. This time, he returned to the storeroom after just a minute.

"The government made an announcement!" he cried, bursting into the room. "They are lifting the curfew for five hours to give people a chance to escape the city!"

Excited, the boys leapt to their feet. Now was their chance to run.

Omar said, "What about the boys' records?"

Mohammad shook his head. "We have no transportation. We can't carry all the files and documents. They'll have to stay behind."

The teachers packed up the few remaining scraps of food in flimsy rucksacks.

"I have to get my brown blanket," Anas insisted. But, of course, there was no time. Besides, it was too dangerous to go up to the second floor. The blanket would have to stay, too. *It won't protect us from mortar shells anyway*, Hameed thought.

"I'm sorry," Hameed told his brother. He could tell Anas was trying to be brave, trying not to cry.

Surrounded by their teachers, the boys filed out of the orphanage. The fresh air felt amazing — and, after the days of constant explosions, a strange silence filled Hameed's ears. The city streets still smoldered in places, and craters pocked the road where the shells had exploded. Hameed didn't know how anyone would ever be able to repair all the damage.

Up on the roof of the orphanage and at the nearby base, the soldiers lowered their rifles and watched them go. A few even waved.

The Taliban fighters must be out there, too, Hameed realized. But thankfully, they didn't fire on the orphans, either. Maybe the Taliban realized that killing more innocent civilians would only further turn the people against them.

The streets were crowded with people taking advantage of the cease-fire, all funneling to the main highway. There, tens of thousands of people clogged the roadway. Cars and trucks honked their horns, maneuvering through the masses of people. Some begged for rides. Others began walking out of the city.

Would the orphans have to get to Peshawar on foot?

"There!" Hameed spotted a bus stuffed with passengers. The bus's roof was nearly empty, though. He could see only a young girl and her parents.

Even so, there wasn't enough room on top of the bus for all fifty of the orphans, plus the teachers.

"We'll split up," Mohammad said. "Omar, you and a few of the other teachers should lead the younger half on the bus. I'll stay with the older children."

Omar looked unsure. "But how will the rest of you get to Peshawar?"

"We'll walk if we have to. There's only a little over four hours left of the curfew. Go."

Mohammad patted a few of the boys on the head, and shook Omar's hand. They agreed to meet up at a UNICEF-supported shelter at the government school in Peshawar.

"Hameed, you come with me," Omar said. "You can help me watch after your brother and the other little ones."

The twenty-five younger boys climbed onto the roof just as the bus lurched forward into the chaos of the highway.

"Hold on!" Hameed told his brother.

They waved good-bye to the other orphans and Mohammad as the bus rumbled slowly away.

✳

Once they were outside Mingora, the traffic eased. In three hours, they had traveled just a few miles. As the sun started to set, the young boys dozed off, leaning against Hameed, Omar, and the other teachers.

Hameed was wide-awake, though, and watched the countryside roll by. This lush, green region had once been enjoyed by thousands of tourists. Now it hosted nothing but overwhelming violence and suffering. Foreigners no longer dared visit, and the area had slipped even further into anarchy.

This paradise on Earth has turned into a nightmare, Hameed thought just as the bus swerved to the side of the road and came to a halt.

Why had they stopped?

Omar jumped down to talk to the driver. Seconds later, he told Hameed and the other boys to climb down, too. "The bus is out of fuel," Omar said. "We'll need to find another way to get to Peshawar."

There wasn't much time. If they were outside when the curfew went back into effect, they could be shot.

The hundreds of people on the road around them seemed to realize the same thing. Those on foot began to run and cars swerved recklessly — everyone was desperate to get away from Mingora. Omar waved at a few cars, trying to get rides for the boys, but none of the vehicles stopped.

A vegetable truck sped toward them, honking its horn and weaving through the traffic.

Omar stepped in front of the truck, its headlights lighting up his scared face. With squealing tires, the truck skidded to a halt just inches from him. The driver and passenger shouted angrily, but Omar hurried around to the side of the truck to talk to them.

After a few moments of frantic conversation, the driver agreed to take Omar and the orphans to Peshawar. They had to make a stop up ahead to wash the peas in the back of the truck. "And I'll need money," the driver added.

Fishing in his pocket, Omar pulled out all the money he could find. "I only have a little," he said.

The driver took all of it and waved for Omar and the boys to climb into the back of the truck. It was a tight squeeze, but they all clambered on top of the pile of peas. Once the boys were all settled, Omar tapped the roof of the truck's cab. The tires shrieked again as the driver pressed the pedal to the floor.

The cool night wind blew around the boys as they huddled together.

"If I had my blanket," Anas said with a little pout, "I wouldn't be cold."

Just a short way up the road, the truck pulled over in front of a small house. The driver got out and started dragging a hose over to the truck. "Everyone out," he told them. "I have to wash the peas, and then we'll keep going."

As the boys waited on the side of the road, Hameed looked around and his heart skipped a beat. "Anas?"

His little brother wasn't anywhere to be seen. Had he wandered off? Was he lost out there in the dark, rocky field beyond the road?

Without a word to anyone, Hameed rushed into the darkness. He had to find his brother.

✱

"I'm all wet!" Anas said, giggling.

He had fallen asleep, snuggled among the peas in the truck's bed, and woke up only when the driver began spraying the vegetables.

As the other boys laughed, Omar couldn't help grinning, too. It was so wonderful to hear the sounds of laughter again. He helped Anas down and gave him an extra shirt from his rucksack.

"Where's Hameed?" Anas asked, once he had changed. "Where's my brother?"

They all looked around, peering into the surrounding darkness. Hameed was gone.

Just then, the driver said, "Hop back on the truck, everyone. Time to leave."

"No!" Anas shouted. "Not without Hameed!"

"Wait, please," Omar pleaded with the driver. "We're missing one of the boys."

The driver shook his head. "I'm going now, with or without you. The curfew will be imposed again soon."

Omar had no choice. He had to get the other boys to a safe place as quickly as possible. He could only hope that Hameed would meet up with Mohammad and the other orphans — or make his own way to Peshawar.

Omar bundled the squirming Anas into the back of the truck with the other orphans. He took one last look around, but still didn't see Hameed.

"All right," Omar finally said to the driver. "Let's go."

That morning, Omar and the boys reached the crowded shelter in Peshawar. It was staffed by Pakistani volunteers and UNICEF workers who provided food, clean clothing, and cots.

"Where's Hameed?" Anas kept asking, with fresh tears in his eyes. Each time, Omar told him, "Your brother will be here soon. He's just running an errand for me."

Three days later, Mohammad led his group of orphans to the shelter. They'd had to walk twenty miles from Mingora before finding a truck to take them the rest of the way. They were tired and hungry. Mohammad and Omar embraced, and the boys from the two group greeted one another, happy to be together again.

Omar checked the older boys' faces, looking for Hameed.

"Oh no," he cried. "Hameed isn't with you."

"What do you mean?" Mohammad said. "He should be here with you!"

Omar described how Hameed had disappeared.

Mohammad asked, "Where would he go?"

Omar thought he knew. "He must be returning to the orphanage."

At around the same time that Omar and his group reached Peshawar, Hameed arrived at the outskirts of Mingora, just as the curfew was reinstated. With government forces on patrol and

Taliban fighters everywhere, Hameed had been forced to walk slowly, traveling in the shadows along the side of the road.

If Anas was lost, he would try to find his way back to the orphanage. Hameed hoped to find him there, and together they could escape to Peshawar.

Overhead, the late afternoon sun blazed, making Hameed an easy target as he inched along the garbage-strewn streets of Mingora. In the distance, he could hear gunfire, and up ahead he spotted figures hovering in a doorway.

Taliban.

Hameed ducked into an alley —

And found himself in the middle of another group of Taliban fighters. There were six of them, each with a rifle. One man carried a grenade launcher. Before Hameed could run, they grabbed him and pushed him to the ground.

"Who are you?" their leader demanded.

"Taliban," Hameed lied. "I'm with you."

The militants shared a look. They didn't recognize him. When they asked which Taliban group he fought with, Hameed's terrified mind could only produce one name: "Mohammad," he said. "Mohammad's group."

The Taliban continued interrogating Hameed into the night. Finally, they tied him up and left him in the alley. In the morning, the leader returned. He untied Hameed and told him to fetch some water. If he didn't come back, the leader said he would hunt him down and make him pay.

Hameed sprinted out of the alley, and kept going. There was no way he'd return there. Not if he could help it.

He ran toward the orphanage, and stopped at the corner. He

peered carefully around it, and saw rifle barrels sticking out of the broken windows of the building and over the top of the roof.

There was one good thing about having the soldiers camped out at the orphanage for those weeks: He had learned their schedules and habits. He knew just the right moment to sneak into the orphanage without being spotted.

And that moment was now!

Hameed ran up the front walk, praying that it hadn't been rigged with explosives. He dashed inside, ran up to the second floor, and into the younger boys' room.

Anas, please be in your room!

Anas's blanket still sat in the corner of the room. Shrapnel had torn through the window and dusted the blanket, burning half of it to ashes.

Let him be okay! Let him be alive! Hameed prayed as he lifted the corner of the blanket.

Anas wasn't there.

Then, once again, Hameed felt rough hands grabbing him.

In the Peshawar shelter, an aid worker had lent Mohammad a cell phone. It took over a day of panicked calls, but he was able to convince the Pakistani military to patch him through to the soldiers' lookout on the roof of the orphanage.

A harried-sounding soldier answered the call. Mohammad began to rapidly explain the situation, but the soldier interrupted him. "You're looking for a boy named Hameed?"

Mohammad said, "Yes, he's sixteen —"

"Yes, yes," the soldier interrupted again. "I know Hameed. We found him in a room on the second floor."

And just like that, the soldier put Hameed on the phone.

"Hello?" Hameed said.

"Oh, son," Mohammad said, tears filling his eyes. "I am so glad to hear your voice!"

"Sir, is Anas with you?" Hameed asked, his words crackling with worry. "Is he all right?"

"Yes, Anas is here in Peshawar," Mohammad soothed. "He's safe. But what about you? Are you okay?"

"Yes," Hameed said. "But the fighting in the city is even worse now. The shooting and the explosions go on and on." Then he added softly, "It's very scary. I'd like to leave."

The soldier took the phone back. "Curfew is in effect. We're giving the boy food and water, but we are not going to let him out."

For four days, Mohammad and Omar made around-the-clock phone calls and worked with the staff of the Peshawar shelter to find a way to get Hameed out of Mingora.

Finally, a major in the Pakistani army agreed to give Hameed a ride. Mohammad and Omar were waiting outside the shelter when Hameed arrived. He jumped out of the backseat and both men wiped away tears as they embraced him.

Hameed noticed one of the boys had made a sign over the door. It said, WELCOME TO THE NEW MINGORA ORPHANAGE FOR BOYS. But how long would they be able to stay here before conflict forced them to run again?

That was a question Hameed would worry about later . . . after he found his brother.

When Hameed hurried into the small structure, the orphans were all sitting on the floor. They were dressed in clean clothes, their hair was combed, and they were eating flat beans and bread.

Hameed's eyes ran over their faces, looking for one. . . .

Someone tugged on his shirt. Hameed glanced down, a smile already forming on his lips. His brother, Anas, grinned up a him.

"You didn't bring my blanket," Anas joked.

"No," Hameed said. "I almost brought it. But then I remembered that you're big now, and you don't need it."

"I'm not *too* big," Anas said and held out his arms. "Pick me up, Hameed."

Hameed laughed and lifted his little brother into the air.

According to UNICEF, Hameed and Anas and the other orphans were relatively safe once they reached the shelter in Peshawar. They received medical care and counseling for the shock from their experiences from therapists provided by a Pakistani charity. Even with this help, the orphans' futures remained uncertain. This account combines different reports from news and charity organizations about the orphans' escape from Mingora. The years of turmoil in the Swat Valley have been especially hard on children. They've witnessed bloodshed and violence — and experienced incredible loss. As long as the conflict there rages on, the suffering of not only children, but everyone in the region will continue.

OPERATION REDWING

AFTER HIS TEAMMATES ARE KILLED IN BATTLE, A WOUNDED NAVY SEAL VALIANTLY FIGHTS FOR SURVIVAL — FINDING REFUGE IN THE MOST UNLIKELY PLACE

The rocket-propelled grenade struck the ground —

And exploded.

The blast knocked out U.S. Navy SEAL Marcus Luttrell. He was blown into the air and sent tumbling down the steep, rocky mountainside.

When he opened his eyes, he saw only darkness.

Was he blind?

No. Slowly, he realized that his battered body had landed upside down in a small ravine. He managed to pull himself out, and took stock of the dire situation.

It was one thirty P.M. on June 28, 2005. His four-man SEAL Team 10 had been sent deep behind enemy lines in Afghanistan. Their mission — code name Operation Redwing — was to capture a ruthless Taliban leader. His name was Ben Sharmak, also known as Ahmad Shah.

The SEALs were to kill the terrorist if they had to. He had ties to 9/11 mastermind Osama bin Laden, and his small army of militants had taken the lives of U.S. marines.

Before they could get to Sharmak, though, the SEALs had come across scores of Taliban fighters armed with AK-47 rifles and rocket-propelled grenades, or RPGs. The bloody battle had cost the Taliban the lives of about thirty-five men. Marcus's three teammates — his friends — were also dead. He'd been cradling one of his mortally wounded buddies in his arms when that last RPG struck.

Only Marcus had survived, and — as he surveyed his wounds on this steep mountainside in the middle of nowhere — he didn't know for how long.

A gash on his forehead dripped blood. His nose was broken. He thought he might have broken something in his back and maybe his shoulder. His pants had literally been ripped off his body by the explosion. Shrapnel and rocks stuck out of his left thigh.

He needed medical attention. Without it, he would bleed to death. But until aid arrived, he would have to help himself.

Luckily, things were quiet for the moment.

Marcus wondered if the Taliban thought he'd died in the blast. . . .

As if in answer, the dirt around him exploded. Hidden Taliban forces opened fire from all sides. But their shots went wild. They must not have known exactly where Marcus was, or even if he was still alive. They were trying to flush him out.

Marcus knew the Taliban killed those who surrendered — so giving up was not an option. Besides, SEALs were not big on surrendering.

Somehow Marcus's rifle had landed next to him. He had a magazine and a half of ammunition left. Dragging himself along the rough terrain, he crawled into a crack between two rocks. He pressed his back against the rock wall inside. His legs stuck out, but were partially concealed by the scrubby bushes that clung to the mountainside.

Small avalanches of rocks tumbled down the mountain as the Taliban forces swarmed around him. Across the canyon, he could see enemy fighters scouring the area for his body.

Marcus had never been so scared in his life. Yet this brave Texan had been trained by the Navy SEALs. And the SEALs took their name from all the places they are trained to operate: sea, air, and land. They endured legendary mind- and body-breaking training to become experts in reconnaissance and direct action missions.

Marcus had never needed that training more than he did now.

Just then, U.S. A-10s and Apache helicopters flew in low over the valley. The choppers must be searching for Marcus's team. They were so close that Marcus could actually make out the features of the pilots' faces.

He could call for help!

Marcus pulled out his radio and tried to speak. But his mouth was so dry and clogged with dirt he couldn't form words. He hit the emergency distress signal button. Someone up there had to notice it!

Over the radio, Marcus could hear the airmen talking to one another. They had heard the beacon! Marcus didn't dare make any further contact — it might get the attention of the Taliban forces around him. He waited for a sign that help was on the way.

But no help came. When the pilots didn't get any further information from him, they must have decided that his call was a Taliban trap, and flown off to search farther down the canyon.

About eight hours after Marcus had awakened upside down in the ravine, the sun started to slip behind the mountains. Darkness settled in.

Marcus would have to do more to get the attention of the

search helicopters. He'd have to take chances that might reveal his location to the Taliban.

He took out two glow sticks, snapped them until they lit up, and attached them to the wires of his radio headset. He spun the glow sticks, hoping the choppers above would spot them.

But it was no good.

Marcus removed the laser from his rifle and pointed it at the next helicopter that swept through the canyon. Nothing.

Now he swung the glow sticks, pointed the laser, and triggered a strobe light he carried. Still, he couldn't get the pilot's attention.

The sounds of the chopper's whirring propeller blades faded off into the distance.

Marcus was alone. Except, of course, for the Taliban forces that were closing in around him.

Marcus needed water. Badly. He'd lost his water bottle during the earlier battle. His dry throat was closing up and he was starting to worry that soon he wouldn't even be able to breathe.

Just then the last rays of the setting sun reflected off something directly across the canyon from Marcus. The barrel of a rifle. And it was held by a Taliban fighter. He swept the rifle across the mountainside where Marcus hid, zeroing in on his position.

Marcus had no choice if he wanted to survive.

He raised his own rifle and shot the man, who tumbled over the edge of the cliff. Instantly, two other Taliban fighters appeared and gazed across the canyon into the shadows where Marcus was hiding. Once again, Marcus had no choice but to fire on the enemy.

He had to get out of the area, before the bodies were discovered.

He packed his radio, laser, and strobe light. Now for the moment of truth. He tried standing up. While the shrapnel in his left leg was unbelievably painful when he touched the flesh, both legs supported his weight.

He jammed his rifle into his belt, so his hands would be free. Moving away from his hiding spot, he started to zigzag toward the top of the steep mountain. The incline was treacherous, and he struggled to keep his balance.

Marcus hoped to find water up at the top, and possibly a good spot for a rescue helicopter to land. Grabbing at roots, branches, bushes, he scrabbled slowly up the side of the mountain.

He was thirstier than he'd ever been. He tried licking the sweat off his arms and sucking on blades of grass — anything to get a little moisture.

When the incline and his wounds made the climb impossible, Marcus changed course, limping sideways across the mountain.

Marcus could hear the Taliban fighters calling to one another through the pitch-black night. They were watching him and moving in for the kill.

Before that fight came, Marcus wanted to make it to high ground. It'd be harder for the gunmen to shoot him from below. He kept struggling across the mountain.

Suddenly he heard the sound of water flowing. At first, his heart leapt at the thought of a long, cold drink. But soon he realized that must be the river where his three friends had died. He couldn't drink there.

He would have to find another source of water.

＊

As the sun rose, Marcus found himself on hard-packed ground. He'd stumbled upon a trail that led to several houses up ahead. He weighed his options and decided it was too dangerous to approach.

He changed direction and left the trail. Hours later, under the baking sun, he heard a stream in the distance —

That was when a bullet tore through his upper thigh.

A sniper had shot him.

The force of the bullet sent him tumbling down the mountainside yet again. Only this time, he landed face-first. For once, though, the steep hill played in his favor: The Taliban snipers had difficulty hitting him as he fell. Their bullets pinged around him, but none of them hit home.

With three snipers firing from above, Marcus crawled for cover. He would have liked to move above his attackers. But right now he could get away quicker by going downhill. Tumbling at times, he scrambled down the mountainside. He finally stopped behind a rock, and waited for his pursuers to catch up. He shot one of the Taliban fighters, then tossed a grenade at the other two.

Marcus zigzagged down the hill for two or three miles. He could hear water again, and then he saw it —

A waterfall set into the mountainside. White clouds of water tumbled into a pool that sat a mile or so above a small village.

It took another two hours to climb to the pool of water. By now Marcus was blacking out from thirst, loss of blood, and exhaustion.

He crawled to the pool and drank. And drank.

Had water ever tasted so good?

He was still gulping water when he looked up —

And saw three Afghans standing over him.

Two of the men had rifles, and the third one was shouting at him.

Marcus crawled as quickly as he could behind a few big rocks.

Why hadn't the Afghans shot him yet? And what was the third man yelling at him about?

He didn't know. He only knew he had to take cover and get in position to fire his weapon.

Before he and his team had been attacked, they'd come across three goatherds. Marcus and the other SEALs had worried the herders would tell the Taliban about them. And after the attack that had cost his friends their lives, Marcus was convinced the herders were the ones who had revealed their location to the enemy fighters.

He wasn't going to make the same mistake twice. He was going to be the first one to fire.

Marcus turned his rifle on the Afghans. Three more had joined the pack surrounding him, all with rifles slung over their backs.

It was six against one, and with just one grenade left, Marcus had little chance of winning this fight.

One of the Afghan men stepped forward.

"American!" the villager said. He gave Marcus two thumbs up. "Okay! Okay!"

"You Taliban?" Marcus asked.

"No Taliban!" He made cutting gesture across his throat with his hand.

After being hunted for nearly a day, it was hard for Marcus to accept that these men might not mean him harm. They were Pashtun villagers, a group that often fed and sheltered Taliban forces.

The man who had spoken smiled. In broken English, he told Marcus that his name was Sarawa, and that he was the doctor in the nearby village. Marcus could tell that the doctor wanted to help him.

Sarawa sent his fellow tribesmen to get water from the pool for Marcus, then took a look at the gunshot wound in Marcus's left leg. When the other Afghans returned, they talked amongst themselves and seemed to come to some kind of important decision.

Suddenly, three of the men lifted the two hundred forty pounds of Marcus's six-foot-five-inch frame.

Marcus tightened his grip on his rifle. With his free hand, he pulled the pin of his last grenade, arming it, and kept it tightly clutched to his chest. If these men tried to hand him over to the Taliban, he would let go of the grenade.

They passed a few other Afghan villagers on the trail. Some of them glared at the party.

What were these men doing with an American? Why were they helping him?

Marcus wondered the same thing as he was carried to the fifteen-hut village of Sabray. Outside one of the dirt-floored homes, Sarawa gave Marcus a drink from a hose. He was safe for now, so Marcus replaced the pin into his grenade, and tucked it back into his battle harness.

With the rest of the villagers surrounding them, the men laid Marcus on a cot. Sarawa examined him and removed the shrapnel from his leg. It was painful, but Marcus was glad for the care.

At about six o'clock, after Sarawa had applied antiseptic and wrapped his leg in bandages, the Pashtuns moved Marcus inside and gave him new clothes.

They served him warm goat's milk, which made him gag. He did, however, eat the flat baked bread they offered. Then the villagers left him alone, trusting him on his own in this home. As the sun set and the temperature plummeted, Marcus was grateful for the blankets — and for the kindness — these people had provided.

He even thought he might be able to sleep. Just as his eyes were beginning to shut —

The door was kicked open and eight Taliban fighters burst into the room.

Someone in the village or one of the Afghans they'd passed on the way there had told the Taliban about Marcus. They stormed over to his cot and began beating him. The villagers had taken Marcus's rifle and grenade. Without them, Marcus could do little to protect himself.

They shouted questions in broken English at him.

"Who are you?"

"What are you doing here?"

"What are the U.S. military planes that fly overhead planning?"

Marcus fed them every lie he could think of. But they kept interrogating him. At one point, he tried to break away. The Taliban soldiers tossed him to the floor and broke his wrist. As they continued to hit Marcus, they taunted him by telling him he had only moments to live.

Then a village elder entered the room, and the soldiers froze. The elder gave Marcus some water and bread, and then spoke very softly — but confidently — to the Taliban fighters.

The men went silent. The elder calmly left the house and soon the soldiers followed him outside.

Bloodied again, Marcus collapsed on the cot, and drifted into semiconsciousness.

Why was he still alive? What had the village elder said?

The door flew open again at about four in the morning. Marcus thought the soldiers were back . . . this time to finish him off.

But no. It was Sarawa with three armed villagers. They picked him up and carried him out of the village into the night.

"Where are you taking me?" Marcus asked. The men didn't answer. They crossed a river and carried Marcus to a cave in the side of the mountain.

Marcus feared they would leave him here to die.

"Back soon," Sarawa promised, and left. Marcus lay alone, shivering in the dark.

Later that morning, the village elder arrived, with more warm goat's milk and some bread. Then Sarawa returned, checked on Marcus's wounds, and posted an armed guard outside the cave.

A long day passed. Marcus still wasn't sure what was happening. Why hadn't the Taliban come for him? Early the next morning, the guard and two others carried him out of the cave back to the village.

They brought him to the house of Mohammad Gulab, the son of the village elder.

Marcus asked for information — what was going on?

With the little English he knew, Gulab told Marcus, "The village will not give you to the Taliban. We will protect you."

Later Marcus would fully understand the importance of the decision Sarawa and the other villagers had made by the river when they discovered him.

They had decided to grant Marcus *lokhay warkawal*, a two-thousand-year-old tradition of defending a guest to the bitter end. Under Pashtun tribal law, the village of Sabray was now committed and honor bound to protect Marcus.

By breaking into the house, beating, and interrogating Marcus, the Taliban had come dangerously close to breaking this custom. If pushed further, the villagers would have no choice but to fight to the death to protect Marcus.

The village elder must have reminded the Taliban fighters of this when he stopped them from beating Marcus. They had retreated that night, but they still lurked in the hills, waiting for their chance to snatch Marcus.

The village elder's son, Gulab, and Marcus became close friends. The language barrier made it tricky, but they were able to communicate.

"I am the policeman in the village," Gulab told him, using a combination of broken English and hand gestures. "I have a wife and six children. And you?"

Marcus tried to tell him about his identical twin brother. But he wasn't able to make the idea of *twin* clear enough. He finally just went with "I have a brother."

At one point, the village children came in and gathered around Marcus's cot. They taught Marcus words in Pashtun, and Marcus taught them words in English. The children also taught him prayers, and at prayer time, he knelt with them, even though the pain in his wounded leg was excruciating.

With Gulab's help, Marcus met with the village's goatherds. Because they spent their days out on the surrounding mountains, they were a good source of information. They helped him figure out how far he'd traveled the night after the battle. They determined that he'd walked, climbed, fallen, and crawled about seven miles.

At night, Marcus was moved onto the roof of another nearby house. Gulab and a guard kept him company and huddled with him for warmth as they tried to sleep.

During the night, Marcus rolled over. Gulab whispered, "Shhhh! You must be quiet! Taliban!"

Still not fully of aware of the power of *lokhay*, Marcus realized then that he was being hidden from the Taliban, and that his presence was endangering everyone in the village.

Two days after Marcus had arrived in the village, the village elder had come up with a plan. He would set out on the thirty- or forty-mile hike to the U.S. military base in Asadabad.

Marcus wrote a note for him to give to U.S. forces: "This man gave me shelter and food, and must be helped."

Marcus was too injured to make the trip himself, and he would be an easy target for the Taliban when away from the protection of the village. So, walking alone, the old man went to get help for Marcus.

Meanwhile time seemed to be running out. A message from a Taliban leader came from the surrounding mountainside. The Taliban demanded that the village turn Marcus over to them.

Gulab assured Marcus that the village's answer was final . . . they would not give him up. They had sworn to protect him and that was what they would do.

In an attempt to repay his new friend, Marcus offered Gulab the only thing of value he had left: his watch. Gulab shook his head, refusing the offer. When Marcus promised him money, Gulab shook his head.

Doing the right thing didn't require payment.

The children of the village spotted the parachuting rescue kit dropped by a U.S. aircraft. It was another sign that the U.S. military didn't know if Marcus was alive or dead — and that they were trying to give him help just in case. The children ran to salvage what they could from the package for Marcus.

The Taliban warriors got to the kit first, though, and forcefully sent the children running back to the village.

Marcus was again shocked by the cruelty of the Taliban.

Going after kids!

Maybe it was a bond of trust they now shared, or maybe they wanted Marcus to be able to defend himself in case of an attack — either way the next morning, the villagers returned all of Marcus's belongings, including his rifle, his combat harness, and his radio.

He pointed his emergency radio beacon out the window of the house where he slept, and hoped it still had enough battery power to reach the helicopters flying overhead.

But instead of answering his distress signal, U.S. aircraft swept overhead, bombing the area around the village.

How did U.S. forces know exactly where to drop the bombs?

Marcus guessed that the Taliban must have recovered the emergency cell phone from the rescue kit — and the United States forces were using that signal to zero in on their location.

None of the bombs hit the village directly. But roofs blew off houses and walls shook. After the attack, Marcus knew the villagers were in greater danger than ever. The Taliban would want revenge. And they wouldn't stop until they got their hands on Marcus.

To help save the village further pain, Marcus and Gulab hatched a plan. The two of them would slip away that night. Marcus would fight the pain of his injuries and follow Gulab through the darkness to a small American outpost a few miles away.

But that night, a driving thunderstorm swept through the area and forced them to abandon their plan. No one was going anywhere, including the Taliban.

The next morning, Marcus sat outside trying to come up with a new strategy, when Gulab ran up to him.

"Taliban soldiers are here in the village!" he shouted. "Run! Run!"

Marcus had left his gun inside, next to his cot. He needed to get it!

But there wasn't time. Gulab half carried him down a hill, and the two men hurried into an empty house. Leaving Marcus there, Gulab ran off. Minutes later he returned with Marcus's rifle and his own AK-47.

Together, they prepared to fight.

In the distance, Marcus heard gunfire.

This went on for a while, until finally things went quiet again. The soldiers must have been frustrated when they couldn't find Marcus, and gone back into hiding on the outskirts of the village.

What to do now?

The village was no longer as safe for Marcus. And they would be spotted if they left for the military outpost in daylight.

Gulab took Marcus to the flattest field in the area. He never said exactly why, but perhaps Gulab knew something that Marcus didn't . . . maybe his father had reached the U.S. military base with Marcus's note. And this field was the best spot for a rescue helicopter to land.

As they waited, Marcus glanced across the field. On the other side, he was stunned to see . . . Ben Sharmak.

This was the ruthless Taliban leader that Marcus and his team had come to capture or kill. And now he and his fighters were right there, partially concealed in the trees. He must have been following Marcus. Or maybe he was waiting for a U.S. chopper to land so he could attack.

Either way, even on the outskirts of the village, Marcus was still protected by the ancient tribal law. Sharmak didn't dare attack — unless provoked.

Marcus raised his rifle and aimed his sights on Sharmak. The Taliban leader saw him, but didn't flinch. Because if Marcus fired, Sharmak's fighters would shoot him, then Gulab — and then who knew how many villagers?

After a tense moment, Marcus lowered his rifle. Gulab made his way over to Sharmak, and the two walked into the distance. Marcus knew they were talking about him.

When Gulab returned, he explained that Sharmak had given him a note that basically said, "If you do not hand over the American, we will kill your entire family."

Marcus was concerned for his friend, but Gulab bravely dismissed the threat. Instead of handing Marcus over to Sharmak, he helped the SEAL up a flight of stone steps carved into the mountainside.

Sharmak and his men didn't follow. They continued to skulk in the surrounding woods, waiting for Marcus to leave the village so they could nab him.

Marcus's wounded, battered body had a tough time climbing the stone stairs. But the trek was worth it.

When Marcus's foot landed on the top step, he looked up to see an Afghan special forces soldier and two U.S. Army Rangers waiting at the top.

He was saved!

The Army Rangers recognized Marcus. One of them pulled him in for a hug, and shouted over his shoulder, "We've got him, we've got Marcus!"

Suddenly, a band of Army Rangers emerged from the nearby brush. Drawn by his emergency beacon, U.S. Special Forces had been searching for Marcus or any possible survivors of Operation Redwing for days.

And now they'd found him.

Marcus was one step closer to escape.

All this time, Gulab's father, the village elder, had continued his long journey on foot. He had arrived in Asadabad, and helped guide the U.S. military's massive air rescue operation.

The U.S. forces hit with a fast and furious air strike on the Taliban forces around the village. Then, that night, they sent in a helicopter to pick up Marcus. He waited in the shadows with Gulab by his side.

As he watched the chopper drop slowly to the ground, Marcus worried the hidden Taliban might fire another rocket-propelled grenade — and dash his hopes of rescue again.

But no . . . the chopper landed safely. The side door was open. Before allowing Marcus on board, one of the airmen performed an identity check to make sure he had the right man.

"What's your dog's name?" the airman asked, using memorized personal information about Marcus. When Marcus gave the correct answer, the airman asked a second security question, "Who's your favorite superhero?"

"Spider-Man," Marcus responded.

The airman nodded with a smile and stepped back. With Gulab's support, Marcus climbed onto the helicopter. Gulab got in behind him. He would make sure his friend made it to safety before going back to the village.

As they lifted off, the airman shook Marcus's hand and said, "Welcome home."

Six days after the launch of Operation Redwing, Marcus landed safely at a U.S. air base, where he and Gulab had to say good-bye. Once more, Marcus offered his watch, and once more Gulab turned it down. "I put my arms around his neck," Marcus recalled to the Washington Post, *"and said into his ear, 'I love you, brother.'" In interviews, Marcus has expressed his gratitude to Gulab and the other villagers who risked their own lives to save his. After recovering from his wounds, Marcus was promoted to hospital corpsman first class, received the Navy Cross — pinned on by President George W. Bush in the Oval Office. Two of his fallen team-mates and friends, Petty Officers Matt Axelson and Danny Dietz, both received the Navy Cross; and the third, Lieutenant Michael Murphy, was awarded the Medal of Honor, the United States's high-est military decoration.*

BENT SPEAR

IN THE MIDDLE OF THE VAST PERSIAN GULF, A SPECIAL OPS TEAM MUST DEFUSE AN UNDERWATER MINE BEFORE IT DESTROYS A SHIP — AND THE NUCLEAR WEAPONS ON BOARD

Tick. Tick. Tick.

The bomb's clock counted down. Troy Weltz needed to clip one last wire . . . and the bomb would be harmless. But he had to hurry. With a steady hand he made contact with the wire cutters, and started slicing through the wire —

A ringing jerked Troy awake.

Instinctively, his hand rose in the air, his fingers working to defuse the bomb from his dream. In a split second, he realized he was in his bed in his stateroom. Not on a mission. Because he was a special operations team leader, Troy's training was always working — even in his sleep.

He snatched up the ringing phone. "Yes?"

"Lieutenant Weltz," a clipped voice said, "this is Captain Hunter, Admiral Frank's chief of staff."

"Yes, sir." Troy sat up straight, instantly alert.

"The admiral wants to see you in the war room." Before Troy

could ask when, the captain said, "Immediately, Lieutenant. Hustle." *Click.* The line went dead.

Hustle? The always proper captain didn't use words like that. And Troy had never even spoken with the admiral, let alone been summoned to a meeting with him.

Dressing quickly, he rushed out of his stateroom into the floating city that was the USS *Patriot*. The sun was just setting and in the distance, two fighter jets soared toward the aircraft carrier like dark birds.

It was late in the summer of 1991, and the Persian Gulf War with Iraq was in full swing. The aircraft carrier served as headquarters for the navy's main battle group, which included an armada of frigates, destroyers, and two ships called AEs that carried extra explosives and ammunition.

The *Patriot* stood twenty stories above the water and was as long as the Chrysler Building is tall — so even with Troy's "hustling," it took him five minutes to reach his destination. As always, Troy felt a rush as he pushed through the door marked WAR ROOM and entered a large, bustling space filled with interactive maps and flickering computer screens.

Admiral Frank was surrounded by his team of advisors. Captain Hunter spotted Troy and broke away from the group.

"Lieutenant Weltz?" The captain sounded surprised and a little doubtful. Troy knew why — he looked much younger than his twenty-eight years. He was used to the reaction, but never wasted time saying anything about it. He just let his successful track record speak for itself.

"We have a . . . serious problem." Hunter was picking words very carefully. "We're deploying you and your team right away."

Troy nodded. "What's the nature of the operation, sir?"

"It involves . . ." The captain hesitated again, and then said, "Special weapons."

Troy could have guessed as much. The term was a euphemism used by the navy to refer to chemical, nuclear, or biological weapons — Troy's special ops team's area of expertise. That was the main reason they were stationed on board — to deal with any sort of special weapons mishap.

"Sir, can you be more specific?" Troy said.

Hunter was struggling for words, when the admiral walked over and cut him off. "We don't have time to dance around facts, Captain," he said, turning to Troy. "Your team, Lieutenant . . . are they good?"

Troy didn't hesitate. "The best, sir."

"They better be," he said, and paused. "We have a Bent Spear."

Oh my God. Troy struggled to keep his face calm as the code words ricocheted around the room like a gunshot.

Now Troy understood the urgency. A Bent Spear meant a nuclear weapon had been compromised or was in a compromised position. And that nuclear device might be damaged. The magnitude of the situation meant that Washington — probably the president himself — was now following the developments.

Admiral Frank let the information sink in, and continued the briefing. "The propeller of the AE carrying the weapons stopped working correctly an hour ago."

"Has the ship been cleared of crew and other weapons?" Troy asked. "My men and I can have the nuclear weapons disarmed by morning. I just need —"

"Morning will be too late," the captain interrupted, tapping a nearby radar screen where a giant dark blob blinked on the edges.

"See that storm? It's packing near-hurricane-force winds. It will be here by dawn. The job must be done now before the seas get rough."

"Understood," Troy said. Leaving the ship unmanned through a storm, with special weapons on board, wasn't an acceptable alternative.

"Not yet, you don't," the captain said. "The nuclear weapons are not what you need to disarm. When the AE's propeller stopped functioning, a diver went down on a short recon mission to find out why. The diver discovered the cable of an underwater Iraqi mine wrapped around the propeller shaft."

"A cable?" Troy asked, stunned. "With the naval mine still attached?"

The admiral nodded. "If that mine detonates, it could blow up the explosives on board that ship, including the nuclear weapons. You need to get over there and fix it, son. Before this patch of the Persian Gulf becomes our worst nightmare."

Troy said, "Aye, aye, sir."

Fifteen minutes later, Troy was on a Seahawk helicopter with the five members of his special ops team.

With their gear prepacked and ready to go, Troy and his team were like firemen — they could mobilize at a moment's notice. Now they zipped away from the aircraft carrier out over the gulf's dark, churning water. The stars on the horizon disappeared as the approaching storm swallowed them up.

He and his men had orders to assess the situation on the AE 32 and call the admiral with a plan of action. Troy had relayed the background of the mission to his team in just seconds. A tight-knit group, they spoke a unique shorthand with one another — kind of like the language Siamese twins sometimes invented to communicate.

"We're not Siamese twins," the youngest member of the team, twenty-year-old Hugh Podeszwa, said whenever Troy made that comparison. "We're closer than that." And in a way, it was true. From eating in the dining hall to planting explosives on Iraqi ships, 99 percent of Troy's waking day was spent with this group.

While the men absorbed the details of their mission, Troy noticed something he'd seen time and time again. As dangerous as this mission was, the faces of the four petty officers sitting across from him glowed. They were excited to take on the challenge that lay ahead.

"This is definitely a wild one," Hal Little yelled over their headsets, his eyes wide.

Vince Mangan fought a smile. "Is it wrong that this is the reason I wake up in the morning?"

"Let's just hope you get to do it again tomorrow," added John "J.D." Dosley.

Normally, J.D. was the team's prankster, but given the danger of their mission, his joke fell a little flat.

"Way to kill the mood, kid," said the senior chief, Oscar Urbania. Troy's right-hand man was a gruff veteran of countless missions. He was eighteen years older than Troy, but moved like an agile teenager.

Hal pointed out the window. "There she is." The running lights of the five-hundred-sixty-foot-long AE 32 looked lonely in the dark as the growing waves hammered the bow. Unable to move on its own, the ship had been anchored to keep its location secure.

Admiral Frank had cleared the area in case things went wrong and set up a distant defensive perimeter around the AE. But Troy knew that miles above, U.S. aircraft were patrolling the airspace while submarines prowled below.

As usual, his team was thinking the same thing. "If just one Iraqi ship or aircraft wanders through . . ." said Oscar.

"Or the storm tosses the mine around . . ." Vince said. "Or we blow it up trying to disarm it . . ."

"Our Bent Spear could become a Broken Arrow," Troy finished for him, using the code for a severely damaged nuclear device. "Bad mojo."

"All right," J.D. said. "Now who's killing the mood?"

The Seahawk made a hard landing on the AE's deck — very hard. The special ops were tossed around the cabin. "Sorry, guys," the pilot yelled. "That last wave was a big one. The deck came to us!"

The AE 32 had a crew of one hundred sixty, though no one could have guessed it that night. The near-empty deck reminded Troy of a ghost ship. The AE had been battened down, the crew enclosed below by sealed hatches. If the mine did explode, hopefully the breach would be contained and the ship wouldn't sink.

While his team unloaded the gear, a seaman led Troy up to the control room and the AE's captain. The night was cool, but the captain's sweat-stained shirt betrayed his anxiety. As Troy shook his damp hand, he didn't blame the captain for his fear. He knew that each wave could be the one that jostled the mine and set it off.

"The area is yours, Lieutenant," the captain said.

"Thank you, Captain," Troy said. "We'll get it back to you ASAP."

Troy took control of the situation like a detective managing a crime scene. He hurried back to the diving platform, where he found Oscar already in his scuba gear. Troy gave him the thumbs-up, and Oscar disappeared over the side of the ship to do a quick recon of the mine.

Five long minutes passed.

When Oscar resurfaced and pulled away his mask, his pale face said it all. They had problems. Big ones.

Troy and his team powwowed in the ship's command information center, or CIC. Plush, high-backed chairs circled a huge glass conference table. But no one sat. The team thought more quickly on their feet.

Oscar had changed out of his scuba gear, but his hair was still dripping as he described what he'd seen below. "The cable of an underwater mine is wrapped around the propeller shaft. The mine itself is pressed up against the hull of this ship."

Hugh lifted one foot off the floor as if his weight might set off the mine. J.D. cocked an eyebrow at him. Hugh blushed and put his foot back down.

"This Iraqi beauty is six feet across and has three activation prongs, like an upside-down tripod," Oscar was saying. "Its seventy pounds of explosives would tear a hole in the ship big enough to drive a car through. And the underwater air bubble created by an explosion could break the back of the ship."

"Thanks for the intel, Chief," Troy said to Oscar. Then, checking his watch, he turned to the whole group. "The clock is ticking, guys. We've got eight hours before the sun rises and that storm strikes. Let's start with traditional solutions."

On top of the usual physical military training, each member of the team had gone through two years of training in explosives, chemistry, and electronics. They had studied the evolution and science of warfare from ancient China to the modern day.

"Obviously, we can't blow the mine with other explosives like we'd usually do," J.D. said. "And cutting it loose from the anchor that holds it in place and dragging it away won't work."

"Yeah," Hal agreed. "Mines are like balloons. If we cut the cable, the mine will just rise up in the water. It will press against the ship and explode."

"Could we open the panel, and go after the detonator?" Hugh asked. "Pull out all the wires and disconnect the power sources?"

No one needed to respond to this one, even Hugh himself. They all knew it was the least desirable option with the highest chance of failure. No diver wanted to have his face in the guts of a mine when it blew.

"Okay, those are the textbook answers," Troy said. "Now let's improvise, adapt, and overcome." That was Troy's favorite special ops motto, the one he lived by. A successful mission often depended on creativity and ingenuity not found in any textbook. "I think we should focus on the anchor."

"Maybe you're onto something," Oscar said, nodding. And together the team built off the foundation of a tiny idea, talking about what equipment they needed, the timing, and who would do what.

The work was intense, and it felt like hours since they'd entered the CIC. But when Troy checked his watch again, he found it had taken six minutes to brainstorm a solution.

"So, men, do we have a plan?" Troy asked, looking around at their faces. They all nodded — what they were about to do had never been attempted, and the team needed to get to work if they were going to stay ahead of the storm.

After explaining their idea to the AE captain, Troy used a secure line to call the admiral and his staff on the *Patriot*. Troy described the situation and outlined their solution.

"Do you remember the question I asked about your team?" the admiral said to Troy when he was done speaking. "Want to tell me the answer again?"

Once again, Troy didn't hesitate. "The best in the world, sir."

"Then you have permission to move ahead with your plan, Lieutenant."

The AE was basically a floating warehouse; it had several different large storerooms on board.

The members of the team, except for Hugh, who had remained in the CIC, made their way to an area storeroom that housed broken equipment waiting for repair. A lone seaman stood guard behind a makeshift desk — a busted surfboard on top of two crates. His head snapped up when the team entered, and Troy could tell he knew who they were.

Even with the hatches sealed shut, word on board a ship traveled fast.

"I think you guys are in the wrong place," the seaman said, and pointed down. "The mine is that way."

Troy shook his head, and began examining a discarded part from a jet engine. The hulking piece of metal looked like it had once been used in a jet's coolant system. "What do you think, Chief?" Troy asked. When Oscar nodded, Troy turned to the seaman, "How much does this weigh?"

"About a thousand pounds."

Oscar gave him a hard stare. "We're going to need you to be a little more exact than that, seaman."

Withering under the look, the soldier quickly checked his computer. "It's nine hundred and ninety-eight pounds."

"Perfect. We'll take it," J.D. announced. "Do you do gift wrapping?"

When the confused seaman didn't respond, J.D. shrugged. "No one has a sense of humor today!"

Troy turned to Hal and Vince. "Find some men to help you get a hand crank attached to the top of this part. Run one end of a steel cable through the crank and attach a C-clamp to the other. Got it?"

They nodded, and Troy radioed back to CIC. "Hugh, how you doing with those calculations?"

"Getting there," Hugh replied. He had an important job — using a sea chart, he had to figure out the exact length of steel cable they needed to attach to the engine part. If his calculations were off, the mission would fail.

"Man, I wish I was the one going down with you," J.D. said, watching enviously as Troy and Oscar suited up in their scuba gear.

J.D. would remain on deck near the dive platform, making sure they had the equipment they needed and relaying their communications to the crew on board.

"I know, J.D.," Troy said. "But we're not using fun toys on this trip anyway."

"And I do love my toys," J.D. said with a grin. He had a fondness for all the special ops gadgets and motorized vehicles the team had at their disposal. But with an impact mine stuck against the ship's hull, Troy was keeping the equipment to a minimum.

On the other end of the ship, Hugh, who had finished his calculations, was working with Hal and Vince. They had welded the hand crank and one end of the steel cable to the engine part, and were connecting it to one of the booms the AE normally used to raise and lower cargo containers.

Troy and Oscar ran through a radio check with J.D. With the perimeter established around the ship, there wasn't too much concern that they'd be overheard by the Iraqis. But with such a sensitive situation, they would keep communications to a minimum.

"We won't need a radio to know something's gone wrong anyway," J.D. said. "The big explosion will be a pretty good indication."

With that, Troy and Oscar splashed into the water and swam the forty feet down to the bottom of the ship. The headlights on their masks were the only illumination in the pitch-black water, giving them short stretches of vision in the darkness.

And there it was.

The six-foot-wide, beach ball–shaped contact mine floated under the ship, its trigger prods just inches from the hull.

"*Gilligan's Island*," Troy murmured to himself. The mine looked like a fake prop from a TV show he'd watched as a kid.

The Iraqis dumped these explosives into the gulf by the hundreds, rolling them off the backs of ships in harbors or along coastal areas. When a mine hit the bottom, it released an explosive that rose to the surface. This explosive stayed attached to the piece of the mine below by a long cable. Sometimes hundreds of mines could dot one small area of the gulf, bobbing in the water like deadly black balloons.

Right now, Troy and Oscar needed to stay away from the mine. Of course that was easier said than done. Deep undercurrents swirled around them, making Troy feel like a leaf in the wind.

"Okay," Troy said into his headset, "lower the engine part."

"Roger," J.D. said. Now that the mission had begun, he was all business.

They'd made a five-stage plan, and this was the most dangerous part of stage one. They'd lower the engine part to the seafloor by a heavy steel cable. For their plan to work, it would have to land almost directly under the ship, which meant they'd have to drop it dangerously close to the side of the hull.

There was a splash as the engine part hit the water. It was coming down too fast and the current caught it. The thousand-pound piece of metal swung toward the mine. Oscar swam between them, like a parent rushing between a speeding bus and a child. The weight could easily push Oscar straight into the mine or crush him against the hull.

"Easy on the descent!" Troy shouted into the radio. "Pull it tight!"

"Roger that," J.D. replied. The cable tightened, and the engine part stopped its deadly swing. Oscar was breathing hard, but he gave Troy the thumbs-up.

The engine part continued its one-hundred-fifty-foot descent, more slowly this time. When it hit the bottom, Troy swam to the surface and called for the other end of the cable to be lowered over the side. This was the end that Hal and Vince had welded a C-clamp to.

Troy grabbed the clamp and swam the cable down to the mine. Hopefully, this would be the only time he would have to touch the deadly explosive. Moving very slowly, he clipped the clamp to a steel loop on the mine, right next to the original cable.

The mine now had two cables attached to it.

Stage two of their mission could begin. They needed to transfer the mine's weight and the tension that kept it from floating away from the old cable to the new one.

Troy left Oscar to babysit the mine and swam down to the bottom of the ocean, following the new cable all the way. The engine part had landed on a slight rise on the ocean floor. Troy's light found the hand crank on top of the engine part — and he got to work.

"Tightening now," Troy said as he started to turn the crank.

Click! Click! Loud metallic snaps sounded around him.

He continued to rotate the manual crank, increasing tension and shortening the length of the new cable. A little bit with each turn. It was agonizingly slow work, but he didn't dare go any faster or he'd jostle the mine. After what seemed like days, Troy paused to glance at his watch. Six hours had passed since they'd boarded the AE.

"We got it!" Oscar announced from above, his voice uncharacteristically excited. "The tension is off the old cable. It's switched to the new anchor line. We're ready to cut!"

This was the moment of truth. Troy swam up to the hull. After checking the tension himself, he attached a homing beacon to the steel loop on the mine. This would allow them to track the explosive later when it was freed from beneath the ship.

But first they would have to sever the original cable. Troy gave the okay to move ahead.

Oscar slowly worked the blades of a hydraulic cutter — basically a high tech bolt cutter — into the cable wrapped around the propeller shaft. If the cutter were to slip in Oscar's hands or if he pulled too hard on the cable, he could jerk the mine into a collision with the ship.

While Oscar worked, Troy ran through the stages of their plan again, thinking through any possible weaknesses or improvements right up to the end. And as he floated near the hull, something popped into his head. He thought of the rise in the gulf floor and how the engine part must be sitting several feet above the mine's anchor.

"Hold up, Oscar," Troy said.

"A little late for that, Troy," the chief said, but he started gently pulling the cutters away from the cable.

"J.D., get Hugh on the radio," Troy said. A couple of agonizing seconds passed before Hugh's voice came over the headset.

"Yes, Lieutenant?" he said, his words filled with static. Troy realized he must be out on deck in the wind. "Are things — "

"Hugh," Troy broke in, his eyes locked on the few remaining steel strands of cable still attached to the old anchor. "Did you take into account —"

"Sorry, I can't hear you!" Hugh shouted. "Did I what?"

"Hugh, don't speak for a second," Troy said, trying to remain calm. "Did you take into account the rise in the seafloor when you made your calculations?"

"Sir —" His voice broke off. Troy's fist clenched in frustration. Without an answer, the mission couldn't continue. Yes, the crank had put the tension on the new cable — but if that cable was too long, that meant they needed to rethink everything.

Before Troy could say anything, Hugh was back, his voice clearer, as if he'd ducked inside out of the weather. "Yes, sir, I know about that rise on the floor! It was on the charts we received from the captain!"

Troy started breathing again. He nodded at Oscar, who cut the last few strands of the old cable.

As it snapped, the mine rose toward the ship. If it hit, they were all dead.

But it stopped after a fraction of an inch. They'd done it. The new cable held the mine away from the hull.

Stage three was complete.

Now stage four could begin. Because the ship's engines still couldn't be turned on with the mine so close, the team had come up with another way to escape the proximity of the mine.

With Troy and Oscar still in the water, J.D. had the captain order his crew to activate the anchor windlasses. These two machines at the bow pulled on the anchor chains and would eventually hoist them out of the water. As the anchor chains tightened, the ship moved forward. It slid away from the mine, which was weighted to the ocean floor by the engine part anchor.

The ship was free!

Troy could hear the cheers from on deck over the radio. The captain was waiting on the dive platform when Troy and Oscar surfaced. The high winds of the coming storm tousled his short hair and he had to shout to be heard.

"Thank you, thank you!" the captain repeated, as he shook each of the team members' hands. "You saved my ship and my crew!"

A tug vessel steamed its way toward them. It would tow the AE out of the area. That was stage five, but they didn't need to stick around to see it.

As Troy and his team headed toward the helicopter that waited to take them back to the aircraft carrier, he slapped his men on the backs and congratulated them.

"Looks like we'll live to see another morning after all, boys," J.D. said, jerking a thumb toward the rising sun.

Troy grinned. "Let's just hope it brings back your sense of humor, J.D."

"Brings *back*?" Hal asked. "How about just brings?"

With the men still laughing, the helicopter lifted off. Troy looked down at the blinking red warning light they had attached to the mine. The explosive bobbed in the waves about a hundred feet off the stern of the AE.

Once this storm passes, I'll be back to take care of you, Troy thought.

And then he turned back to celebrating with his team — the best in the world.

The following day, the lieutenant and one member of his team went back to destroy the mine with a timed explosive. After the first Gulf War concluded in 1991, the members of this special ops team were recognized in a private military ceremony for the work they had done. One of the most memorable moments of these amazing events, according to the lieutenant, was shaking the admiral's hand after returning from the AE and hearing him say, "Well done."

ACKNOWLEDGMENTS

While writing this book, I had the honor of speaking with a few true American heroes. They generously took time to recount their experiences, even when it meant enduring the pain linked to those memories. I am deeply grateful for that privilege — and for the permission to shape their stories as necessary for this book — and I would like to thank Mark DeCorte, Crystal Kepler, Chris Duke, and Timothy Faust. Thanks to Mike Teesdale of the United Kingdom.

Any errors in this book are strictly the fault of the author.

I would like to acknowledge the role that Marcus Luttrell's book, *Lone Survivor: The Eyewitness Account of Operation Redwing and the Lost Heroes of Seal Team 10*, played in writing "Operation Redwing." Lutrell's astonishing courage and his commitment to preserving the memory of his fallen teammates are awe-inspiring.

For those looking for more information on children in need in Pakistan's Swat Valley, UNICEF.org makes a good starting point.

For her patience, support, and eagle-eye editing skills, my ongoing thanks to Jenne Abramowitz at Scholastic Inc.

Also, my appreciation goes out to Susan Cohen at Writers House, Tom Doyle, John Doyle, Mike Doyle, Dan Kirk, Dave Dutch, Paul Dutch, Jivana Esposito, Brianne Johnson, Andrew Baharlias, Nan Vincent, and Riccardo Salmona.

And, most importantly, my biggest thank-you is for the men and women who have served and are serving so bravely in our country's military.

SELECTED BIBLIOGRAPHY

Blumenfeld, Laura. "The Sole Survivor." *Washington Post*, June 11, 2007. http://www.washingtonpost.com/wp-dyn/content/article/2007/06/10/AR2007061001492.html

Gordon, Michael R. "A Platoon's Mission: Seeking and Destroying Explosives in Disguise." *New York Times*, July 12, 2006. http://www.nytimes.com/2006/07/12/world/middleeast/12military.html?_r=1&scp=1&sq=a+platoon%27s+mission%3A+seeking+and+destroying&st=nyt

Gretarsson, Alistair Ingi, and Shandana Aurangzeb Durrani. "Reaching Conflict-affected Orphans in Swat Valley." UNICEF, June 1, 2009. http://www.unicef.org/infobycountry/pakistan_49857.html

Lanham, Fritz. "A War Hero from Huntsville Rues a Decision Made in Afghanistan." *Houston Chronicle*, July 2, 2007. http://www.chron.com/disp/story.mpl/front/4936654.html

Luttrell, Marcus. *Lone Survivor: The Eyewitness Account of Operation Redwing and the Lost Heroes of Seal Team 10.* With Patrick Robinson. New York: Little, Brown, 2007

Naylor, Sean D. "Surviving SEAL Tells Story of Deadly Mission." *Navy Times*, June 18, 2007. http://www.navytimes.com/news/2007/06/navy_sealbook_070618w/

United States Department of Defense. "Petty Officer 1st Class Marcus Luttrell." Heroes. http://ourmilitaryheroes.defense .gov/profiles/luttrellM.html

United States Department of Defense. "Technical Sergeant Mark DeCorte." Heroes. http://ourmilitaryheroes.defense.gov/profiles /decorteM.html

United States Navy. "Lt Michael P. Murphy USN." Medal of Honor, USN Recipients. http://www.navy.mil/moh/mpmurphy/ index.html

Watson, Ivan. "Lost Boys of Swat Flee for Their Lives." *CNN.com*, May 13, 2009. *http://articles.cnn.com/2009-05-11/world/orphans .swat.taliban.pakistan_1_orphanage-taliban-mingora?_s= PM:WORLD*

ABOUT THE AUTHOR

Bill Doyle is the author of *Behind Enemy Lines: True Stories of Amazing Courage* (Scholastic), the Crime Through Time series (Little, Brown), and *Attack of the Shark-Headed Zombie* (Random House). He's also written for the American Museum of Natural History, *Time for Kids*, and *Rolling Stone*, among others. He lives in New York City and invites you to visit him online at www.billdoyle.net.